To Vicky —
with love
and a deep sense
of sharing —
with this book

Moonbeams and this
Come at stage of life.
Dark Times

Enjoy the Moonbeams
mine & yours.

Susan White-Bowden
May 29, 1993

Other Books by Susan White-Bowden

EVERYTHING TO LIVE FOR
FROM A HEALING HEART

Moonbeams Come at Dark Times

Turning Fifty in the '90s

SUSAN WHITE-BOWDEN

 GATEWAY PRESS, INC.
BALTIMORE   1992

First printing, 1992

Please direct book orders and all correspondence and to:
WHITE-BOWDEN ASSOCIATES
2863 Benson Road
Finksburg, MD 21048

Library of Congress Catalog Card Number 92-73517
ISBN 0-9633762-0-9

Cover Photos: Marjorie White. All rights reserved.
Front: Susan White-Bowden with granddaughter
         Emily by fish pond. Summer, 1992.
Back: Susan White-Bowden with grandchildren. Fall, 1991

Moonbeam drawing by Bruce Rydell
Cover and Text Design by Janet Kratfel
Typsetting by The Desktop Shop

Produced for the author by Gateway Press, Inc.,
1001 N. Calvert Street Baltimore, MD 21202

Printed in the United States of America

Dedication
To My Mother

...for all the things I didn't understand, or say, while she was alive. For example, the year she turned fifty was the year I turned sixteen. At the time, I thought my mother was old, and out of touch. Now I realize what a vital young woman she must have been at that age, and how much energy, understanding, patience, and personal fortitude it took to deal with some of the problems and worries I caused her that year.

Special Thanks
To my husband Jack Bowden

...for the support and encouragement that has always been a part of our relationship and for the advice and first stage editing on MOONBEAMS COME AT DARK TIMES. Without Jack this book would have been much longer, with fewer commas, and far fewer moonbeams.

To Connie Clausen — my literary agent, mentor, friend, and second stage editor. Connie gave this book it's shape, and suggested it's title.

Contents

Introduction   xi

Chapter One

The Good Life   1

Second Honeymoon   3
You Don't Look Like a Grandmother   8
Working at home   10
Out of the Mouths of Grandchildren   13

Chapter Two

Keeping the Nest   15

Helping Husbands   17
Cleaning the House   20
A Room of My Own   25
Lingerie Drawer   28
Significant Other   31

Chapter Three

Looking Good   37

Shopping   39
Thin is Always In   41
My Diet   43
Vacation Fitness   47
Working Out   49

Something's Cookin'   51
Dinner Party   54
Out of the Mouths of Grandchildren   59

Chapter Four

For the Love of Children   61

My Son's 30th Birthday   63
Play with Me   65
Love   67
Stepchild—Love's Stumbling Block   69
Pets are like Children Too   72
Out of the Mouths of Grandchildren   80

Chapter Five

Forever Someone's Child   83

Role Reversal   85
Daddy's Little Girl — Mother's Daughter   100
Mother's Day Tribute   102
Volunteers   104
Self-Esteem   109

Chapter Six

Seasons and Off-seasons   115

The Wonders of Winter   117
Ski Trip   119
Dining Room Table   125
Easter Egg Hunt   127
State Fair   129
Off-Season   131
Inconsiderate Drivers   133
Out of the Mouths of Grandchildren   136

Chapter Seven

"Grand" Mother Nature   139

Earth Day   141
Fish Pond   143
The Outer Banks   146
May Flowers   148
Out of the Mouths of Grandchildren   150

Chapter Eight

Looking Inward   153

A Time to be Selfish   155
Being Alone   160

Chapter Nine

Age of Acceptance   163

Out of the Mouths of Grandchildren   165
Tina Turner Turns Fifty   167
Meta Joy Turns Fifty   169
Let's Talk   171
Growing Old Gracefully   174

Chapter Ten

Health Watch   177

Come What May   179

Chapter Eleven

Looking For Moonbeams 195

Winter of Discontent 197
Watching a War on TV 203
Flag Waving — Peace Weaving 208
Thinking Brings Direction 212

Chapter Twelve

Spring 1991 221

Spring Preview 223
The Moonbeams of Spring 227

Chapter Thirteen

Making Every Day Count 233

Reunion 235
Summer Camp 239
Giving Thanks 247

Conclusion 251

Introduction

In thinking about youth and what we all go through, it seems to me, even today, under the best of circumstances, with the finest relationships in the most secure young families, the twenties and thirties of a person's life are the most difficult and stressful years. It is at that time in life when we experience the most demands on our time and energies, and, it seems, our always less than adequate finances. That is when our relationship with our spouse needs the most commitment; when our children need the most attention; when our boss is the most demanding. We have to work hardest during that period in our life to prove ourselves. It is when we make the least amount of money and need to spend the most; to pay for housing, cars, health care, and eventually education for our kids.

It is when there is a powerful passion for everything from careers to sex, that propels us almost uncontrollably in search of success, satisfaction and security. Our passion seems overwhelming at times and can send families and relationships into a tailspin, if priorities aren't established early on.

The joy of being young includes high levels of energy and enthusiasm for new experiences, from romance to marriage to giving birth. Our health is usually better, we weigh less, and our ambitions are higher.

Even so, I wouldn't go back to my twenties and thirties, if it were possible, because I've worked hard and labored long to get over the hill and I like this side of life's mountain much better.

As I think back over the first fifty years of my life, it often seems like someone else's life. Perhaps it is because I've tried to forget so much. I hope it's not because senility is setting in. Memories are fading, and are a little easier to take.

When I do look back it's like looking at old photos of myself and thinking, "How could I have ever thought that style was becoming?"

When you think about what many women, who are turning 50-years-old in the '90s, tried to accomplish in our 20s and 30s, you realize that it was darn near impossible to do, and yet we did it. We set out to conquer the world as our mothers knew it, and ended up changing it to the world that our daughters live in today. It's no wonder many of us are so willing to publicly declare that we're now membership material for the AARP. After what we went though in our youth, it doesn't hurt a bit to acknowledge that we are no longer young. It's not only a relief. It's a profound pleasure.

What we sought, as proper young women of our time, was the ideal life. We wanted to become the perfect wife, mother, housekeeper, hostess, and community volunteer. And later we decided to become liberated, to make our mark in the world of business. We went after jobs that only our brothers would have pursued before.

We demanded equal pay with our male counterparts, often going without the support or help of our husbands. Support which many young women, who successfully combine careers and families, have today.

"When I was seventeen it was a very good year," croons Frank Sinatra. Well, when I was seventeen I had gotten myself into an early marriage and dropped out of school. I already had one child with another one on the way. A third would be born by the time I was twenty. My life was diapering and dusting and trying to be a good mother, a job for which I had neither training nor maturity. That was the daytime me. At night I took on the role of understanding companion, lover, and hostess with a never fading smile or unfailing recipe.

When I reached twenty-five I realized I was not (never had been) comfortable in my role, or content to make it my life. I became restless and started to look for fulfilling experiences outside my home. And thus began the struggle to balance home and children and career. It was a struggle that would last for a decade and end in divorce.

Years later tragedy struck not once but twice. My ex-husband committed suicide and then, two and a-half years later, my beloved 17-year-old son, Jody, followed his father's example and took his life. The death of my son was almost more than I could endure.

An on-going outreach to other parents and teenagers across this country through personal contact and with my first two books, *Everything to Live For*, Poseidon Press, 1985 — Pocket Books, 1987, and *From A Healing Heart*, Image Publishing, 1988, has helped me to survive.

I have gone on with my life — but it's impossible to experience such tragedies without having them affect your life forever.

I have learned that no one goes untouched by problems and the pain of loss. Perhaps that's why when we live through these personal ordeals and arrive at a less stressful time, it can be the most rewarding period in our life.

When I hit forty my life really changed and started to become fun. I was beginning a new, exciting, yet comfortable marriage with my best friend. I had established myself in a career, I felt good about who I was, and what I could and should do with my life. I became a grandmother with ease; no pain; no strain; no medical bills, only the pleasure of seeing, and showing off what I felt were the smartest, most beautiful babies ever born.

And then I hit fifty and with it discovered how fabulous life can really be. I didn't even mind the hot flashes because they came mostly in the wintertime. It's not that there aren't problems, I just seem better able to handle them, or I don't take them or myself as seriously as I did when I was young. And I'm less likely to create problems for myself. I'm so comfortable with my life now that I'm not even tempted to flirt with some handsome young man at a cocktail party. And secure enough to believe that if I did he'd respond. Now that's being satisfied with one's station in life. Don't you agree?

I know not all women in their fifties are experiencing the joy of life that I am. I know that because I've talked to women who are not, and I've seen other women who are not, on Oprah, Donahue and Sally Jessy Raphael. Their stories break my heart and make me realize how lucky I am. Their husbands have left them for a younger woman. They have been forbidden to see their grand-children. They have lost their jobs because of age. There are many outside forces to get in the way of what can be a wonderful period in a woman's life.

But there are hundreds and thousands of women, just like me, who are convinced that "it doesn't get any better than this." I've seen *them* too: in the supermarket with their grandchildren, at the zoo, or in the park. I've seen them on vacation, with their husbands of many years, rediscovering the love that brought them together and kept them there, through some pretty difficult, as well as rewarding times.

And there are women, with new husbands, who are discovering how exciting new love can be at this, or any age.

And there are women alone, or with other women, a la "The Golden Girls," who have learned the depth and security of their own being and the importance of friends.

And so it is from that perspective that I now write. A new perspective of enjoyment, humor and appreciation of life that I've never known before. Who knows how many springs are left on my calendar. We can't know, but I'll tell you this; I'll make the most of each one, without looking back, or ahead. Perhaps because of the pain of the past, and the uncertainty of the future, the present looks pretty darn good.

What follows is a collection of essays that were written and broadcast on my daily radio show during the year 1989–1990. Some have been rewritten and expanded for print, some are new, done specifically for this book, all have helped me sort through particular problems and pleasures of being middle-aged. I hope you enjoy them as much as I enjoyed the experiences, and writing about them. They are a reflection of my life now; the laughter and the tears; the fun and thoughtful perspective of a woman who is finding fifty a whole lot better than I ever thought it would be when I was twenty-one.

During the course of compiling and writing this book I learned that fifty, like any other age in one's life, is not a panacea. But throughout those difficult days that you'll read about toward the end of the book I tried to keep in mind what my granddaughter helped me realize in her profound innocence.

Emily was five at the time. She had drawn a picture. It was dark with streaks of yellow. The kind a psychiatrist might get you worried about.

Emily wanted to title this picture but since she couldn't spell the words she asked me to do it for her.

"Okay," I said, crayon in hand, "you tell me what to write, and I'll write it."

Without hesitation this child of five looked at me with her big brown eyes and said:

"Moonbeams Come At Dark Times."

I stared at my granddaughter in astonishment, and slowly repeated what she had said.

"Moonbeams Come At Dark Times?" She nodded her little head yes, and smiled.

She had not said "Moonlight Comes At Night," as I might have expected, but "Moonbeams Come At Dark Times."

As I wrote her words on her picture I thought, "Oh my lovely Emily, they do indeed. You couldn't possibly have any idea of the depth of what you've just said."

I looked into her angel-like face and realized that she had been just such a moonbeam, that had come into my life, during the dark times following my son's suicide.

1 The Good Life

A husband who likes being
married to a grandmother.

Second Honeymoon

My husband Jack and I were huddled together like a couple of excited kids, looking out of the airplane window at Bermuda's welcome mat of transparent blue water, coral reefs and pink beaches.

It was the year I turned fifty and we were going back to Bermuda for our tenth anniversary.

It had been on our honeymoon, ten years earlier, in this island paradise, that we began to discover what a really special relationship we had; that what we would experience, as a couple, would be very different than either of us had ever known before.

For example, I used to ride motorcycles, "trailbikes," with my first husband, my two daughters, and my son through the woods around our property. After my first husband's death, my son, Jody, and I often spent time riding the trails together. Occasionally we'd take a picnic lunch along; find a peaceful spot at the nearby lake, and share some serene moments. Those times were much needed then, and cherished memories now.

As a result of my cross-country motor-cycling experience I was very comfortable on the Bermuda mo-peds.

Jack had never ridden a motorcycle or mo-ped, and he had no desire to ride one. Adding to his apprehension, the Bermuda newspapers were filled with reports of tourists being hurt in motorbike accidents. It didn't seem safe or sane to him to go out on those small winding roads, crowded with cars, buses, trucks, and inexperienced moped drivers, who were also trying to remember to drive, the British way, on the left.

However, I convinced him that I was a good driver, and he consented to ride on the back of my motor bike. I drove and he held on. So secure is he in his masculinity, this brand new husband had no problem clinging to the little woman, attracting the stares and then smiles from all, as we flew by.

When we decided to return to Bermuda for our tenth anniversary it was a spur-of-the-moment decision, and we couldn't get reservations at the hotel where we had stayed on our honeymoon. Disappointed but not deterred, we took a suggestion and recommendation from the travel agent, about another one.

It was wonderful. We discovered a new part of the island, a new place that we hadn't even seen on our first visit. We fell in love all over again, with each other, and the island. It all seemed so new, the hand holding, the hibiscus flowers and morning glories intertwined together in the hedges along those narrow road ways, exploring the shallow waters and small secluded beaches of Somerset, holding this man that I loved in ocean water as blue as his eyes, the cliffs of coral, white roofed cottages, and a sky to match the sea.

We didn't ride the mo-peds, or even do much sightseeing. Each day we sat on our secluded beach and talked; we read and wrote and realized, too quickly, that the sun was setting and we'd hardly done anything. Certainly not all those wonderfully interesting things we talked about doing over breakfast.

What made our tenth anniversary trip to Bermuda even more like a honeymoon than our honeymoon were the ten years in-between. During those years we had learned that the person each of us had fallen in love with, and married, was someone we really liked, and respected, and cared about — more than we cared about ourselves. We had shared a lifetime of events in that decade. We had gone from co-anchoring a television newscast together, to Jack being fired and my resigning because of it. I felt compelled to give up a twenty-two year career, that could have gone on, because of how unfairly he was treated. I was so unhappy and emotionally distraught, after he left the station, that I just couldn't continue in a job that I loved.

My grandchildren were born during that decade, and Jack's son graduated from high school. My book, *Everything To Live For*, about the suicide of my 17-year-old son, had been written and published during those years.

The process of reliving the tragedy in order to write about it, and then to relive it over and over again when out on a nationwide book tour was grueling, and took an emotional toll on me. The rewards were the hundreds, perhaps thousands, of people, many of whom wrote to me, who were helped to avoid such heartache as a result of the book and my speaking out on radio and television and in newspaper articles.

During those first ten years of our marriage my father and mother, both in their 80s, died.

I experienced the shock of having my mother die suddenly of a heart attack, and then I went through the ordeal of seeing my father lose his independence, following a stroke. He lived for two years after the stroke, and though we kept him in his home, he needed round the clock care. He could no longer drive or get around with ease as he once did. He was a dentist, who continued seeing patients right up until he had the stroke at age 82. At the end he lost his wife, his health, his dental practice, and his will to live. It wasn't easy to watch that happen to someone who had been so strong all his life. There was a complete role reversal; he became child-like, needing my care, and I became parent-like, giving the care.

After ten years jammed with the highs and lows of life and death, love and loss, Jack and I needed that anniversary trip to Bermuda, and it was as perfect as any vacation could be. That was partially due to where we stayed, but mostly because of the comfort we had developed in our relationship.

At one point during our stay Jack took my hand in his and said, "I hope you aren't offended by this, but I'm so comfortable with you."

I wasn't offended, because I have learned that the most beautiful, exciting or desirable thing in the world

— man, woman or island — is so much more enticing when it's enjoyed in an atmosphere devoid of pressure and pretense; when one feels comfortable.

And so it is with the life I now live. Whether it's on vacation in Bermuda or at home on the farm in Maryland, I'm comfortable and at peace in my world.

You Don't Look
Like a Grandmother

In 1983 I became a grandmother for the first time. With the birth of Emily Beth Timchula, a new, much needed, and welcomed joy was born into my life. An unconditional experience of love and wonderment without the day to day, exhausting responsibility of raising a child. Yes, I think the good Lord knew what he or she was doing with the implantation of that biological clock in women. Full time mothering IS for the young.

Since 1983 my two daughters and their husbands have provided me with five more grandchildren, all boys, for a total of six with whom I have begun to relive life. When people find out that I have all these grandchildren the reaction is usually the same.

"I can't believe it, you don't *look* like a grandmother," they say, meaning it as a compliment.

I realize that those words are meant to be kind, but hey folks, to borrow from Gloria Steinem, this is what grandmothers look like these days. They're youthful, and active; involved and productive, at home, as well as in the community. *AND they are sexy.* I'll bet that some of the attractive women in your office are grandmothers. They are doctors and lawyers, businesswomen and hospital volunteers. I even know a policewoman and medic who are grandmothers.

The image has changed. It can be, and often is, the most productive period in a woman's life.

Yes, as we approach the twenty-first century, there is more to being a grandmother than baking chocolate chip cookies. Besides, we've already taught our grandchildren to do that for us.

Working at Home

"So what is it you're doing these days," people ask.

"I'm working out of my home," I say.

"Doing what?" the questions continue.

"Well, I'm writing and broadcasting and producing videos, all on a free lance basis. Jack and I started our own business."

"Don't you miss being on TV every day?" they say.

"Oh no," I say, and I mean it.

We have choices in life, and I've traded the big bucks of TV for a less stressful way of life.

On a recent warm sun-soaked day, when we should have been up in the office tending to business, Jack and I were standing on the porch overlooking the garden. "Are you going to plant morning glories to grow over the trellis again this year?" he asked.

"I did that yesterday," I said with a devilish laugh.

"I can see you really miss going to the TV station everyday," he said, pleased that his wife was happy.

"No way, José. There *is* life after TV and we've found it."

The only problem with working out of one's home is the telephone. People tend to call at all hours, day and night, and early in the morning, on business.

Several weeks ago the phone in our house rang at 6:45 am. The phone is on Jack's side of the bed so he answered it in a startled, groggy state. The person calling asked to speak to me. Jack passed the receiver across the bed with one of those looks that said, "If I'm irritable all day it's your fault."

On the phone was a superintendent of an out-of-state school district. He said, "I apologize for calling this early, but I know how busy you are and I just wanted to make sure I got you." This reportedly intelligent, educated man was calling to confirm a speaking engagement I had made months before, that wasn't scheduled to take place for another month. Now, one of the reasons I like working for myself is because I can schedule my own day. No boss does that for me. And I never begin my work day before eight; nine and ten is even better. Whenever, I like to make some sort of schedule and stick to it. But that's tough to do when your office is in your home. People tend to forget that even though someone may conduct business out of their home they do have a personal life. So I thought for my sanity and self-preservation, and the sake of my marriage, and for others in the same situation, I should set down a few guidelines . . .

Business hours are nine to five whether you work in a downtown office building or in the home.

Some people conduct business on Saturday, check to find out.

Never call on Sunday or holidays.

Of course one of the joys of working for yourself is that personal calls can be made and received anytime without disapproving looks from some boss. Even during business hours, when I'm trying hard to be disciplined and do my work, I welcome calls from friends and family, especially from the grandchildren. As my own boss I tell myself grandparenting is very productive, and is an important part of my present job description. Besides, a phone call with a little voice on the other end *always* brings a smile, no matter how early, or how late.

Out of the Mouths
of Grandchildren

I'm very fortunate.

All of my grandchildren live nearby. My daughters and their families, my husband and his son and I all live on the same family property, that was originally bought by my grandfather.

I was given the old farm house. My daughter, Marjorie, inherited my mother and father's home and my other daughter, O'Donnell, was given a piece of the property on which she and her husband built the third house on the ninety acre farm.

It's a wonderfully unique situation that allows me to see my grandchildren almost everyday, if only for a few minutes while they're out at play.

It is also a situation which can be a little exasperating at times for my daughters when I go against the rules to spoil my grandchildren, even more than *I* think is reasonable. My husband, Jack, tries to keep me in line, but it doesn't always work, especially when he's not around to comment or glare.

For example — it was 5:00 p.m. and 3-year-old Tommy and his 5-year-old brother Jay had come into my house to say "Hi" and ask for a piece of candy; mostly to ask for the piece of candy.

"It's almost your dinnertime," I said, trying to be responsible.

"I don't think you should have candy now." I continued my reasoning.

"It's not dinnertime," said Tommy, not understanding the concept of time.

"We'll eat our dinner," said Jay, who did understand both the concept of time and my concerns.

"Okay," I said, giving in as they both knew I would. "But, just one piece. Your Mommy isn't going to be happy with me when she finds out I gave you candy this close to dinnertime," I said, preparing them for a possible reprimand when they went home with chocolate-smeared faces.

Tommy turned around, looked up at me with his irresistible smile, lips lined with chocolate, and said, "I'm happy with you, MeMe."

2 Keeping the Nest

An immaculate house is a sign
that I'm in someone else's home.

Helping Husbands

Since Jack and I both now work out of our home, we are sharing the office duties as well as the household chores, and he's getting much better about doing his share of the cooking, cleaning and laundry. However, as with most men his age, who grew up with their mothers doing it all, there is a lot of room for improvement. Even younger, liberated men could use a little training.

A recent survey revealed that in most marriages the burden of responsibility for keeping the house clean and doing the laundry still rests squarely on the weary shoulders of the wife and mother who, also, often works outside the home.

I think the problem lies with men not knowing what to do or when. And I just don't think they see what we women see.

For example, when we're getting ready for company my husband always asks what he can do to help. Jack is a very willing helpmate. I'll say, "just look around and see what needs doing and do it." But he couldn't possibly see what I see. The newspapers remain scattered around the living room. The vacuum cleaner sits quietly in the closet. The dust goes undisturbed on the tables. But then fifteen minutes before our company is due he begins cleaning out the medicine cabinet.

I wouldn't lie to you, that actually happened. I came running down the hall, through the bedroom, and into the bathroom to make sure all the towels were nice and neat and there spread out across the top of the vanity were all the things that had been in the medicine cabinet, hidden from critical view, behind a closed door. Now, with our guests due any minute, Jack was standing over the bottles and band-aids and bunches of cough drops, busy washing the empty shelves of the cabinet. He whistled contently as he worked.

"What are you doing?" I asked as calmly as possible, trying not to show the panic that was gaining ground.

"I'm helping," he said proudly.

And they wonder why we have headaches. Well, at least I can find the aspirin now.

When our guests left that night Jack turned to me and said, "I wonder if anyone noticed the medicine cabinet?" We both laughed, The panic, pre-party pressure, and headache had long since disappeared, replaced by the warm glow of wine and a gratefulness that Jack had gotten everything back in the medicine cabinet before everyone arrived.

The experience taught me a valuable lesson. After that, when Jack asked, "What can I do to help?" I'd say, "Nothing, please there's nothing left to do." Our medicine cabinet hasn't been cleaned in a year.

However, just the other day I read in the newspaper about another survey that disclosed that 90 percent of the people who go into other people's homes look in the medicine cabinet.

Maybe Jack knew what he was doing. Maybe Jack is one of those people. "Jack!" I yell, "I could use some help with the housework. I think our medicine cabinet is long overdue for a cleaning."

"Why," asks Jack, "is company coming?"

Cleaning the House

I must admit my views on housecleaning have changed a great deal over the years. I was thinking about that on our tenth anniversary trip to Bermuda. There are many things about a luxury vacation to love, not the least of which is having someone else do the cleaning and daily chores to tidy up the nest: running the vacuum, cleaning the bathroom, making and changing the bed everyday, which always seems a bit unnecessary to me. But I have to confess that when I crawl between clean sheets every night, which always start out firmly tucked in, I know I'm on vacation.

As I sat on our veranda, in that island paradise, overlooking the post card view, I heard the sound of a vacuum cleaner behind me. Did it destroy the dream-like ambiance? Quite the contrary. I felt peace and a sense of order sweep over me. There I was not lifting a finger, and yet I knew that when I walked into my room it was going to look as if "House Beautiful" were coming to take pictures.

I don't know about you, but I'd love my house to look that way, all the time, everyday, and it hardly ever does anymore. We make an effort to try and achieve that look whenever company is coming, but that is the only time. On a daily basis I've gotten more tolerant, more forgiving of the family's messy living habits.

I've learned to walk by a pair of smelly tennis shoes in the living room, and not pick them up and toss them, without looking, into my stepson's room. "After all," I say to myself, "what's more important, a neat living room or a stepson who feels comfortable living here." "Don't answer that," I tell myself, "you'll be sorry when he gets married and moves out."

I guess I've gotten more tolerant with age, or is it lazy? A little of both. I no longer think it's worth the daily hassle to have a spotless house; not worth the physical effort to do it myself, nor worth the mental anguish to nag others to do it.

There was a time when I quietly did daily chores, just like the hotel maid. I dusted and straightened everyday. I vacuumed, even when it didn't need doing. I washed the shiny white, non-yellowing kitchen floor every Monday and Friday. I even did windows.

Now, at this stage in my life, my house is lucky if it gets vacuumed once a month. I'd rather arrange flowers. It's fun and artistically rewarding; besides, when people come in they notice the flowers and not the dust.

My friend Kitty told me the secret of "a clean house with little effort," years ago. I didn't listen to her then, because I thought I had to conform to my grandmother's work schedule.

My mother had a part time maid, but even so her house wasn't as orderly as my grandmother's. I liked the way my grandmother's house looked better.

However now, looking back, (through bifocals, without the line, of course), I realize that though I liked the look of my grandmother's house, I preferred living in the house my mother kept. Once, when I was a little girl visiting my grandmother, she gave me some of her fresh baked cookies, but told me not to eat them until I left. She wrapped them neatly in a paper napkin, twisted very tightly at the top. She didn't want me to eat them there and get crumbs on her nice clean rug.

My mother had a sign in her kitchen, "This house is clean enough to be sanitary, but dirty enough to be comfortable," and it was. But as a young bride I tried to keep a house as my grandmother had. Besides, and more to the point, it's the way my first husband wanted it to be kept.

Monday was wash day, which meant, of course, changing the sheets on all the beds.

Tuesday I ironed.

Wednesday I did windows or walls; the extra things that needed doing, like polishing brass or silver and worst of all, cleaning the oven. I think the greatest invention of modern times is the self-cleaning oven.

Thursday I shopped.

Friday I did regular cleaning.

And though my grandmother didn't do it, Saturday for me was lawn and garden day.

And on Sunday, well the Lord might have rested on the seventh day, but women like me who were seeking a perfect home and surroundings, didn't. There was always something more to do.

For example, every night of the week, after the children were bathed and fed and put to bed, I would put their toys neatly away. Of course, now I know that I should have made them do it. But back then I felt I needed to do it all. Every toy soldier, every stuffed animal, doll and game of a hundred pieces I would put back in the proper order.

My friend Kitty used to come to my immaculate house and shake her head. "You work too hard," she said, not criticizing but sympathizing with someone so willing to accept this sanitary lot in life. "Now the first thing you should do," she said, "is get a rug for the center of the kitchen floor. A hooked or braided rug is best; something loosely woven with gaps in it. When the dirt is tracked in through the back door and into the kitchen it'll usually end up on the rug. Eventually the dirt will sift through the rug. Every few weeks lift up the rug and sweep up the dirt. In the meantime no one can see the dirt because it's hidden under the rug. And," she went on, "if you find other things to do to keep your mind occupied, even you'll forget that the dirt's there."

My friend also gave me another time saving tip, which I ignored at that time.

She said, "In the hallway, or anywhere else you have hardwood floors or any hard surface flooring, if you wait long enough, and don't clean every week, you'll find that, just like gritty teenagers, dirt and dust balls have favorite gathering places. You'll find the grit and grime congregating under the hall table or behind an open door. When you see it pile up, get a wet paper towel and wipe it clean."

Some women are wise beyond their years and we should listen to them. Finally, I have taken Kitty's advice, and I now thank her for it. I wish I had taken it sooner.

When I worked full time in television I hired a cleaning lady to come in once a week. I saw it as a necessity rather than a luxury, since most days I worked ten hours or more. And I could well afford to pay someone then.

However, since leaving full time employment, myself, I've gone back to doing my own housework. But following Kitty's lead, I've come up with dozen's of time-saving cleaning tips that have allowed me to completely disband my former cleaning schedule.

For instance, I now wipe the mirror in the bathroom clean after a shower when it's already fogged with steam. And I take a few minutes to clean the tub and shower before getting out. I keep a spray cleaner on the side of the tub.

Even so, my house has never been as clean as it was when I was young and just married. But my life is more orderly now and a lot more interesting, and don't forget I have a helping husband and a very clean medicine cabinet.

A Room of My Own

There's a little room in my house. It's on the second floor, in the back, and it's very quiet.

I call it the pink room, because it's painted the palest shade of shell pink I could find. It has two dormer windows that face the east. The morning sun filters through flower print curtains of soft muslin.

There's a three-quarter length antique spool bed made of walnut. I had to have the mattress and box spring specially made to fit the unusual size.

The bedspread is cotton eyelet, of old ivory. The pillow coverings are a fine cotton with lace and hand embroidery trim. They're very old. They were my mother's and her mother's before her.

There's an old pine wash stand and an over-stuffed chair and ottoman of sea foam green.

In this room, I call mine, I have my treasures. There are old family pictures in antique frames; my parents and grandparents; my brother and me when we were children. There are more recent pictures of my children and grandchildren.

There is art work and handmade gifts from my grandchildren that I want to save.

There are letters and cards that I just can't throw away.

There are a few very special books that I'm going to re-read. Though I'm very protective of this room of mine, often, when one or two of the grandchildren are staying overnight I let them sleep in the old bed. We look at the old pictures and I tell them about the people in those photos, and how they are related to them. And I tell them stories of when I was a little girl.

This is also a room where I can go to get away from the world. And since everyone knows that it's my room, and no one goes in without my okay, it's almost magical.

For you see, unlike the rest of the house, when I open the door to my little pink room everything in there, all my treasures, are exactly where I left them. They haven't been moved at all.

The tie-backs on the curtains are adjusted just so. The pictures, carefully arranged on the pine wash stand remain in place. The pillows are still fluffed. The little soft off-white lambswool blanket is neatly folded and lying just where I put it, over the left side of the chair.

It's wonderful to have a room all your own. When problems and chaos invade the rest of my life, the rest of my house, I can go to my room where I find peace and order. I can look at my past and get a glimpse of my future, that hopefully I'll live to enjoy with the help of this room. A room where I can go to retreat, reflect, and to unjangle my nerves.

Lingerie Drawer

My mother had this lingerie drawer that was always a mystery to me as a child.

It was a big, deep drawer in her bureau and it was filled with old yellowed night gowns, saggy slips, and stretched girdles. She liked the stretched girdles because she said they were comfortable. She wore the comfortable ones when working outside in the garden. My mother believed that a lady always wore a girdle no matter where she was or what she was doing. She tried to teach me the same restricting philosophy, which I rejected by the time I was twenty.

Most of the things in that drawer she no longer wore, except the stretched girdles, and the few newer things on top. Two full length bras, one white and one black. Two half-slips, one white and one black; one new, hardly worn, very firm girdle, and several pairs of nylon hose.

One whole corner of this drawer was filled with old nylons that had runs in them. Mother wore the ones with runs when she was working around the house and out in the garden, because, not only didn't a lady go around with a jiggly bottom, she also didn't go bare-legged.

The mystery to me was why she kept all those other old things that she never wore.

But low and behold I now find that I have a lingerie drawer just like my mother's. It's filled with things I'll never wear again. What happens is that you buy new lingeries, mash down the old, place the pretty fresh things on top and close the drawer.

Well, I've decided I'm going to clean out my lingerie drawer. I'm only going to keep the things that I'm now using. I'll keep the panties that fit me, not the bikini ones that might fit again someday. I'll keep only my favorite flannel night gown and the long cotton one; out go those skimpy lacey things that I put on once in a while to be seductive, usually on evenings my husband falls asleep right after the news, the *early* news, and I end up freezing the rest of the night.

On second thought, maybe I'll keep just one, the black one or the sheer white one.

We can't dash all hopes in a lingerie drawer.

But all the rest go. It's time for a clean start.

Who needs all these reminders of the past? That nightgown that I wore, for a few minutes, on my wedding night.

The one I wore as I held my first child to my breast.

The push-up bra that I wore once with that low cut dress, when I was trying to regenerate interest in a waning relationship. It didn't work.

The taffata slip I wore under my wedding dress when I was a bride for the second time at age 39.

And what's this?

It's what's left of a much-loved, much-dragged, baby blanket.

Well, maybe I'll clean this lingerie drawer tomorrow.

Perhaps I now understand why my mother never did.

Significant Other

Have you ever thought of living in the country? Have you dreamed about finding a charming, old house, fixing it up and living with history? Well, I did that thirty-some years ago, so I feel qualified to offer this advice. After you find the house that captures your imagination and steals your heart; a house in just the right rural setting; before you get carried away with the romance of it all; before you check out the area schools, or local services or shopping facilities; before you even tell your husband or children that you have found the dream house that will be perfect with just a "little" work; before you do anything else, do yourself a big favor, and scout the area for a plumber with whom you can establish a long-term, close, intimate relationship. Because if you don't, not only are you going to be living with history, you're going to be living with leaky pipes.

Now this can't be just any old reliable, capable plumber, it has to be one with whom you're really comfortable. Because this relationship with your plumber is going to become almost more important than the one you have with your husband. Marriages don't always endure. The relationship with your plumber must. You're going to be calling this significant other in your life in the middle of the night, even on holidays. There will be impassioned phone calls that could easily be misinterpreted by someone who doesn't understand, like someone who lives in a modern condo in the middle of the city. "Hello, Larry, you've got to come now! Please, please, I need you right away! My water's broken again." My plumber has heard that statement many more times than my obstetrician. Your plumber is going to be a friend and psychologist, your hero *in* a white charger, that usually has the name of the plumbing company painted on it's side.

So remember, before you buy that old house, be sure to look for the plumber with whom you may be sharing the rest of your life.

In recent years there is another person who has become even more significant than my plumber. He's the man in my life who found me a new plumber when Larry became disabled with a bad back, and went out of business.

Gil is a former forest ranger who's now in business for himself, helping city slickers who have moved to the country. He helps them determine the difference between manure and mud pies — which to spread — which to throw — and which one smells so "gol darn" bad. He mows fields, plants lawns and trees, digs ditches, plows snow, and pulls legs better than anyone I've ever met.

Gil would just as soon work quietly and efficiently alone, but if you insist on helping, he'll let you. It's his form of entertainment, the chuckle he gets at the end of the day when he's long since gone home, and you're still trying to figure out if you've been had.

For example: in a dry monotone that gives no hint of what he's thinking, whether he's serious or joking, he might ask you to hand him the end of a rope that lies coiled on the ground. You reach down for the end of the rope closest to him and place it in his outstretched hand. "No," he says shaking his head with some impatience, "The end of the rope, not the beginning."

One young man, intent on helping Gil, spent most of one day trying to find a hose shrinker. By the time the naïve youngster returned, without the hose shrinker, Gil had cut the hose and it was securely in place. The man apologized for not finding a hose shrinker, explaining that he had tried everywhere, the hardware store, even the fire house. Leaning back against his truck, Gil took a long drag on his cigarette, and as he exhaled he said, without a trace of a smile, "You're due to be married soon, aren't you son?"

"Yes Sir," The boy said proudly. "You'll find it then," Gil said, as he patted him on the shoulder, got in his truck and left.

Since I've taken over most of the responsibility of running and caring for our farm I've come to rely much more heavily on Gil's help, knowledge and experience, and to lean on him as a dear friend.

As with any *true* friend there are no pretenses between Gil and me. He's seen me at my best and my worst, and he's been known to point out the difference.

One spring morning he arrived early to plow the garden. I had just stepped out of the shower when I heard the tractor running up near the barn. I threw on a terry cloth robe and ran out with bare feet and wet hair to show him exactly where I wanted the garden to be.

"You going out?" He asked. "Yes," I answered, "I have a spreaking engagement at ten."

He looked into my un-madeup face, framed by the straggly wet hair, and said, "You better get going. It looks like you've got a lot of work to do before you leave."

Gil has single handedly kept our 18-year-old riding lawn mower operating. Most of the time. After the years of time and work he's invested in that mower I now tell him it's part his. When something goes wrong, which is pretty regularly, I call and say, "*Our*", meaning his and mine, "lawn mower has a problem." He says, "Everytime I hear that word "our," I feel like I'm pregnant."

But, like a good expectant father he comes when he's called and breathes life back into the old mower.

One summer morning he pulled into the barnyard to begin replacing the carburetor on the mower. I knew he was coming and I had been watching for his truck. He had barely finished pulling back the tarp to uncover the mower before I was standing by his side. He looked into my face and saw I had been crying.

"The pony didn't make it." I choked out. "She died last night. She's down in the stall."

I had called Gil the night before to tell him that the lawn mower wasn't working, and that the old pony had taken a bad fall while running down a muddy hill to be with the other horses. The vet said that she hadn't broken anything, but that there might be internal injuries.

"Well," Gil said, pulling the tarp back over the mower, covering it up again, "I guess we're going to bury a pony today."

"I was hoping you'd say that." I said, "I just couldn't bear to have that pony hauled away to the glue factory."

Gil went home, loaded up his tractor and backhoe, trailered them over to my place and spent several hours digging a grave in the pasture while I spent most of the day crying and trying to figure out how I was going to get myself together enough to comfort the grandchildren when they came home from school, and were told that the old pony, whom they loved dearly, had died.

It was almost sunset when Gil reloaded his tractor and backhoe to take them home. He had not only provided a much needed service, he had also helped us all get through a very difficult day. He talked to the children in such a kind and wise way. He stayed to watch as we sowed wild flower seeds on the top of the grave that he had smoothed over with such care. And he had even carefully removed one of the pony's horseshoes before he buried her so we'd have a part of her to hold forever.

As he was leaving I asked how he had intended to spend that day, other than putting the carburetor on "our" lawn mower.

"Oh, today's my day off. Since I work most weekends I try to take Wednesday's off." I looked at him in a apologetic way.

"Never mind," he said, understanding how grateful I was. "There'll be another Wednesday next week."

3 Looking Good

Let's be reasonable about this.

Shopping

You know that you're going through a change of life when you go shopping and bypass the latest silks and cotton prints, the little black cocktail dresses and sequined sweaters, to buy a sweat shirt with cut-off sleeves that will be perfect over an old faded pink turtle neck and baggy green sweat pants.

I've never been much of a shopper, but I did like nice clothes. I still do. The problem is I've reached an age, and a stage, I never thought would come to me. I feel as if I already have something to wear, no matter where I might want to go. This is a complete reversal from the way I used to view my wardrobe. I'd stare into my jammed closet and find nothing suitable to wear, at least nothing that didn't need ironing.

Thirty years ago my mother used to say, "Susie, go buy yourself a new dress and let me pay for it."

"No, Mother," I'd always say, right before I went shopping. "Why don't you get something new for yourself?" I'd urge.

"I don't need anything," she'd say, "Besides I like to see new things on you. They look so much better on you than me."

Now, at age 50, I know how she felt. When I do push myself to get a new outfit, for some special occasion, like a wedding, I hate trying on clothes.

"Maybe I'll come back when I've lost ten pounds," I tell the sales girl. She looks at me with doubt. We both know that the bride-to-be will be on her second marriage before that happens.

I find it much more enjoyable to go shopping if I don't have to take off my clothes. I haven't bought a bathing suit in five years. I'd much rather buy clothes for other people in the family, like my grandchildren.

However, the other day, I did see a suit I liked. It has a pencil straight skirt and if I can convince the store to let me buy the size twelve jacket and size sixteen skirt I'm going to take it.

In the meantime, I can't wait to get back into my sweats.

I realized how lax I've become about my clothes after a conversation with my 4-year-old grandson, Tommy. His mother, my daughter Marjorie, was giving a baby shower for her sister-in-law and I had been invited. On the day of the shower Tommy was over at my house before the party was to begin.

"I guess it's time for me to get dressed for the party," I said to Tommy. "What do you think I should wear?"

He thought a minute, looked up at me and said, "I guess a dress. Do you have a dress?"

Thin is Always In

There I was standing in the checkout line in one of those uptown, up scale super markets, balancing three, not one, but three boxes of those very fancy, very fattening desserts they sell. We were having company. It wasn't all for me.

There I was staring around the dessert boxes at the magazines on sale, all with beautiful, thin, very thin, women on the covers. Next to the pictures of the thin models in bold eye catching print were the titles of the latest fad diets.

"DROP FOUR POUNDS NEXT WEEK WITH OUR NO FUSS DIET."

"48 HOUR DIET MELTS FLAB AWAY." That one probably turns you loose with Eddie Murphy and Nick Nolte. If you survive you lose weight. Two magazines side by side — one says, "20 POUNDS IN 20 DAYS"; the other says, "20 POUNDS IN TWO WEEKS WITH OUR SPICE DIET." It's come to that, a big Mac means lots of McCormick spice.

The American dream, to be thin, sure sells magazines. However, it is unrealistic to think that any of us standing in that checkout line, with or without three boxes of desserts will ever look like the women on the covers of those magazines. But it's human nature to want to and magazine publishers are counting on that.

Elise Chisolm, writer for the *Baltimore Evening Sun*, once asked a leading fashion designer, who had brought his clothes to town for a charity fashion show, about this issue. She asked why his models were *all* so pathetically thin, why he didn't have at least a few models who looked a little more like the women in the audience. He said, "Women don't want to look at women who look like them. They want to look at women who look like they want to look."

It sells clothes and magazines. It's why there are thin young women reading the news on TV and not well rounded middle-aged ones.

But you know something, first lady Barbara Bush has brought style and respectability to size 16, as well as grey hair, and I say let's elect her president next time.

My Diet

Like most women, larger than size 8, I've tried many diets over the years. The diet closest to my normal eating habits was handed to me by a friend, as a joke. She said, "Now here's a diet you can live with." I read it and said, "This is the diet I do live with."

Here's the diet.

BREAKFAST — half a grapefruit, slice of whole wheat toast, small glass of tomato juice.

LUNCH — broiled chicken without the skin, spinach, 1 oreo cookie, herb tea.

MID-AFTERNOON SNACK — rest of package of oreos, 1 quart Rocky Road ice cream, 1 jar hot fudge.

DINNER — large pizza, 2 loaves buttered garlic bread, pitcher of beer or bottle of wine, 3 Milky Way candy bars.

BEDTIME SNACK — entire frozen cheesecake eaten directly from freezer.

Here are the diet tips that keep me on target with this diet.

1. If no one sees you eat it, it has no calories.
2. If you drink a diet soft drink with a candy bar, they cancel each other out.
3. Food eaten to make you feel better such as chocolate, brandy, or anything with the name Sara Lee, doesn't count.
4. Movie related foods, such as popcorn and Milk Duds don't count because they are simply part of the entertainment experience.
5. Cookie pieces contain no calories, the process of breakage causes caloric leakage.
6. Anything that doesn't go on a plate before going into your mouth is not fattening. That's why I love cocktail parties with all those delicious hor d'oeuvres and dips.

There is one side affect to this diet that I feel I must warn you about. If your husband catches you in the kitchen after ten p.m. with a mouthful of cheesecake or chocolate ice cream not only does your body pump up, your face turns bright red.

On the somewhat serious side, and weight can be serious, I have learned a few helpful things about diets over the years. These tips have helped make it possible for me to wear about the same size clothing for the past ten years. (No matter what you do, bodies have a way of rearranging themselves as the years go by.)

I learned that fad diets don't work. You always put the weight back on, usually with a little extra.

I learned that starvation isn't the answer. That causes your metabolism to slow down and you burn fewer calories.

I used to rush out of the house in the morning without eating anything. I would be so busy running around doing interviews for my nightly television reports, writing them, and then going on the air, I hardly noticed I hadn't eaten. I rarely felt hungry. Some days the first food I consumed was about 7:00 at night. Often on those days I actually gained weight. The reason, I have since found out, was because my metabolism shut down during the day, then the heavy meal I ate at night just sat there and turned to fat.

A small nutritious breakfast of cereal, milk, and fruit, or a scrambled egg, wheat toast, with a glass of tomato juice gets the human, calorie burning, furnace started. Small, healthy meals throughout the day keep it going. The secret is keeping the calorie intake small but frequent.

Combine that with the physical exertion of a normally active life, plus some sort of regular exercise routine, like walking, and you'll have a good chance of maintaining what I call a respectable weight. You'll also feel pretty good, want to be more active. I think perhaps that's the best reward of all.

Understand and accept, as I now do, that no matter how much you diet or exercise you will never turn a St. Bernard into a poodle. I'm certainly not as thin as I'd like to be. There are those ten to fifteen pounds I'd like to lose to put the fun back in shopping. I'm also not as heavy as I might be if I ate large portions at irregular intervals.

If I cut out the wine in the evening I'd have this health thing under complete control. But we have choices, and I choose a few extra pounds for the pleasure of a mellow sunset.

Vacation Fitness

I find vacations the best time to try and take my own advice about eating right and getting in shape. For me, it's easier to concentrate on my physical needs and well being when I'm on vacation than at home.

It's more pleasant to exercise in beautiful surroundings, to swim and play tennis at a lovely resort, that was built for such leisure activities, than to try and do it at home during a busy work week.

I also find it easier to watch my weight, to eat sensibly, in a restaurant, than when cooking for myself. When I'm in the kitchen I nibble a lot, which doesn't stop me from eating a full meal with the rest of the family. It's also more exciting to eat low calorie food in a restaurant. Grilled chicken and caesar salad doesn't seem like diet food, especially when it's served on fine china by a handsome waiter.

Vacation exercise can also be painless, luxurious, and bring about an uplifting feeling of time well spent. It's wonderful to start getting in touch with a body that once was. To feel the muscles tighten, to draw in the stomach and actually see it move. To put your hands on your waist and feel a waist rather than rolls of fat.

There I was, early in the morning in the hotel pool, swimming through the water like Esther Williams, stretching my arms, smoothly kicking my long legs, gliding through the water like a dolphin, and feeling as thin as an eel. Yes, vacations do allow us the chance to fantasize, and to act out those fantasies for a few days.

Just one bit of advice while you're living this fantasy, rediscovering your youthful body in just one week. Don't get out of the pool and walk into the locker room without wearing a coverup. You might catch a glimpse of yourself in a full length mirror, and believe me, that can not only shatter an illusion, it could ruin your whole vacation.

Working Out

May has been proclaimed national physical fitness and sports month. In May of 1990 on the south lawn of the White House, with the help of Arnold Schwarzenegger, President Bush declared war on the couch potato. Well, I'd like to declare war on the couch potatoes who get up only to go to the gym to workout.

As President Bush was watching Maria Shriver's muscle man husband demonstrating his physical abilities, the President turned to his grandson and said, "If Arnold can do that, why can't you pick up your socks?" Exactly! Thank you, Mr. President. I could hear mothers and wives and stepmoms all over America cheering. I know I did.

The men in my household, my husband and his 19-year-old son, have a real thing about staying in shape. They both have shoulders and biceps of which to be proud, made perfect by visits to the gym several times a week.

At the gym those shoulders lift weights, push up, pull out, and whatever else one does there to look like that. It's good for them and they look great, but I keep telling them they can achieve the same results by working out at home. I'd like them to expend the same energy, enlarge the same muscles, while reducing my list of chores.

Instead, at home, those same shoulders can usually be found horizontal on the couch in front of the TV, or vertical in a chair supporting a nodding head.

Above the head of the one with the young shoulders lying on the couch, in his room on the second floor, (and I *do* mean on the floor), are socks, sweaty tee-shirts, and dust under the bed.

Outside there is grass to mow, trees to trim, and fences to mend, not to mention a house that needs painting.

When this is mentioned, the eyes in the head that's attached to those powerful young shoulders open, then so does the mouth, which says, "Yeah, I'm going to get to that, right after I go to the gym to workout."

Something's Cookin'

In spite of trying to stay fit and watching our weight Jack and I love good food and we both enjoy cooking. We even devise and occasional recipe that's worth messing up the kitchen for.

One such creation, recently entered in a charity cooking competition, was named a winner by judges the like of New York Times food critic Craig Clairborne.

The dish is Cream of Maryland Crab Soup. It was derived from combining the two most popular crab soups in our area.

Maryland Crab Soup is a red soup with a clear broth. It's made from vegetables, and steamed Chesapeake Bay hard crabs. This is a spicy hot, robust soup. It's Jack's favorite.

Cream of Crab is a white cream soup, similar to cream soups made with clams or lobster. It's my favorite.

The difference between the two crab soups resembles the difference between Manhattan Clam Chowder and New England Clam Chowder.

One summer I decided to use some left over hard crabs to make soup. Trying to please the taste buds of both Jack and me, the idea struck me to combine the best of both recipes. The result, "Cream of Maryland Crab" soup. It's wonderful, and if you don't want to take my word for it ask Craig Clairborne.

The peppery seasoning off of the steamed crabs makes it a very spicy soup. If you like it extra spicy add a teaspoon or two of hard crab seasoning, such as "Old Bay," right from the can.

When creamed the tomatoes, peppers, and hard crab seasoning produces a lovely shade of salmon, making it a very pretty, eye appealing soup.

Jack and I never had a child together, but we have Cream of Maryland Crab soup to brag about.

CREAM OF MARYLAND CRAB SOUP

1/2 dozen steamed and seasoned hard crabs (picked)

1 cup chopped onions

1/2 cup chopped celery

1/2 cup chopped parsley

1/2 cup chopped fresh red peppers

1/2 cup chopped fresh green peppers

3 large fresh Maryland tomatoes

1 stick of butter

2-3 tablespoons flour

1-2 quarts of milk

Saute onions, celery, parsley, red and green peppers in butter in soup pot. When tender, add crab feelers and claws for flavor. Cut tomatoes in chunks, add and simmer, remove skins. Add picked crab, stir gently. Add flour, stir carefully. Add milk SLOWLY for desired consistency. Bring to a boil, serve hot. For added fun and flavor add hard crab feelers and cracked claws to nibble on while you eat the soup.

Cooking hints: I never use a recipe. I constructed this one for the Cooking Competition. So play around with it to suit your taste. If you like lots of peppers or onions, add more; if you don't like them at all, leave them out. If you want to add extra crab meat, put it in. The thickness of the soup is determined by how much flour you add. If you like a heavy cream soup, add extra flour.

Dinner Party

If there's any doubt in your mind that children copy what they see adults doing, in person, on TV, and in the movies, let me tell you about a dinner party held at my house recently.

It was a spontaneous affair, and aren't those always the best. I had promised my 7-year-old granddaughter, Emily, that she could have her friend, Jennifer, over to spend the night. Since Emily has three brothers and two male cousins who are her primary playmates every day, I thought it would be fun for her to have some "girl time" away from the boys. Well it didn't exactly work out that way, although at bedtime she and Jennifer were alone together giggling themselves to sleep.

When Jennifer arrived all the boys were hanging around: Brian, David, and Jay, all five years of age at the time; Tommy, who was three, and Alexander, who was two. All the boys were looking kind of forlorn because they hadn't been invited to the overnight at MeMe's. I also had second thoughts about excluding the boys from the entire evening.

Concerned about the hurt feelings, as the boys listened, I suggested to the girls that they have a dinner party, and invite the boys.

"Yeah, that's a great idea," squealed the girls, as the boys came crashing through the back door.

"No, No, No," I yelled, putting out my arms to stop the forward motion of these midget linebackers, "Not yet, you're invited for dinner at 5:30. The girls have to set the table, bake cookies, fix the hamburgers, and get dressed. Come back at 5:30," I instructed. One of them asked, "When's 5:30?"

I looked at the clock. "In an hour," I answered, wondering to myself how we girls were going to accomplish all that in just one hour.

I gently pushed the boys toward the door. Once outside I called to their mothers, who were standing nearby talking. "The boys are invited to dinner at 5:30. Emily and Jennifer are having a party."

"Oh, that's great," one says, pleased for her children and delighted not to have to fix dinner herself.

Back inside, I began to direct the budding hostesses. Based on many, many years of experience in last minute entertaining I got the girls revved up and into gear to prepare for this party without panicking about the limited time.

There's a fine line between productive adrenalin flow and disastrous overflow, and I've crossed the line on occasion. One time I was sure I was having a heart attack. I wasn't. I didn't collapse, unfortunately my souffle did.

Emily and Jennifer set the table out on the screened porch, as far from prying adults as possible. I gave my consent and encouragement to the location. This was a meal destined to produce more than normal mess. In such cases the porch brings less stress for me.

Next the girls got dressed, in grown-up clothes that I keep in a trunk in the kid's playroom. The two dresses they chose were former evening gowns of Emily's Mother, cut off to be floor length for 7-year-olds. When they came down to bake cookies, already dressed for dinner, I suggested that the order should be reversed, next time, no time to back track now.

Adding aprons to the outfits, they baked tollhouse cookies from scratch. They read the recipe and did it all themselves, with a little help from me to explain 1/4 and 3/4, and the difference between tablespoon and teaspoon.

All the while we could see the boys circling the house and peering in the windows, trying to see what was going on that they weren't a part of. At one point all the boys disappeared. When they came to dinner we found out why. At their mothers' suggestion they too had decided to dress for dinner.

At 5:25 the cookies were baked, the hamburgers were on the grill, everything else was on the table, and the girls had headed for my make-up.

"We'll also need something to put around our shoulders," said Emily. "It might be chilly on the porch during dinner," she continued in a grown-up way.

I got out two woolen stoles which they wrapped around their delicate young shoulders. They glided off to the porch, heads held high in what they assumed was a manner of sophistication, to greet their guests.

When the boys arrived they were scrubbed down, dressed up and smiling about it. It's hard to stereotype anyone these days. There was a time when no self-respecting boy would have willingly looked this way. The boys wore dress shirts and clean pants. They had not only combed their hair, they had parted it, and slicked it down with water. Jay's cowboy boots were shined to a mirror glaze, and David wore suspenders, or braces, as I'm told they are now called.

The girls seated the boys and asked what they would like to drink

From that moment on the girls were in charge. They served the dinner, and policed the party as well. At one point, mimicking their mothers, Emily and Jennifer rushed to the kitchen to report that David was mis-behaving, he wouldn't stay seated. So, they had decided that he was not going to be allowed to have any cookies for dessert.

I suggested that being a gracious hostess didn't include doling out punishments to uncivilized guests. I explained that if guests were really bad, you just didn't invite them back.

When I began this dinner party idea I thought it would be just that, a dinner party and no more. But at the end of dinner, one of the girls decided that it should be a dinner-DANCE, again, surprisingly, the boys went along. They did slow dancing, holding one another, arm in arm, cheek to cheek. And they did some arm twisting, body twisting, rock and roll.

Now remember these are 2-, 3-, 5- and 7-year-olds. I had to keep reminding myself of that.

The party took on an even more alarmingly adult look when the boys started pretending to draw draft beer from a keg. They'd walk into the hall, hold an imaginary glass under an imaginary spout, pull down on the pretend handle and get a tall cold imaginary beer, which they'd then carry back out on the porch to drink while talking to the girls.

During the course of the evening I realized that it had gotten much too quiet on the porch, I went to check. I found that all the kids had gone upstairs to the bedroom, off of the playroom. Normally, that wouldn't have bothered me, but after that pretend beer I wasn't sure what was going on. To my relief I found that their adult fantasy was over; they were just rough housing in the way children their age do.

I had declared that the party would end at 7 o'clock. The boys were to go home, and the girls would continue their overnight. At seven my daughter O'Donnell and her husband Steve came to get their three boys. The 5-year-old twins, Brian and David went reluctantly, but they did head for the door, as their parents had directed. However, 2-year-old Alexander, who usually clings to his mother in new social situations looked up at his mother and said, in an assertive tone, "Go home, Mommy, we're having a blast."

The age of innocence is getting closer and closer to ending, as well as beginning, at birth.

Out of the Mouths
of Grandchildren

Fall was flirting with the fading summer season. After a very long, very hot summer the cooler temperatures felt good to some and down right cold to others.

I was caring for the twins, 5-year-old Brian and David. They wanted to go out and play. I said they could but that they needed to put on the sweaters their mother had left for them to wear.

Brian obediently put on his sweater.

"I don't need a sweater," said David.

"Yes you do," I said, opening the door to make sure. "It's cold outside today. You'll freeze to death," I lectured, exaggerating, as I often do.

"MeMe," said David impatiently, "why do *I* always have to wear a sweater when *you're* cold?"

4 For the Love of Children

The pain of the past can open
our eyes to the joy of the present.

My Son's 30th Birthday
March 8, 1990

It was a Tuesday, a lifetime ago, and a blanket of deep snow covered the countryside. I had spent much of the preceding weekend sledding with my two little girls. Marjorie was almost 4 and O'Donnell was just 16-months. Any parent who has taken children that young sledding knows that they slide down the hill and *you* pull them up the hill. That is probably why I was heading for the hospital on March 8th, 1960, a week before the due date of my third child. But whether Jody White was born that Tuesday or a week later, he was definitely a Tuesday's child, full of grace and fair of face. A cherub with a head full of blonde hair. "He's too pretty to be a boy," I would hear over and over from friends and relatives as they admired the new baby. And then as Jody grew, and his sweet nature was revealed, I would hear,

"He's too sensitive to be a boy. He should have been a girl."

After his death by suicide at age seventeen I heard it again, "Jody was much too sensitive for a world like ours. A boy has to be tougher than a girl to survive." I didn't believe that then and I don't believe it now.

Jody was sensitive, but he was also strong and rugged. The problem was that Jody was told that it was wrong for a boy or man to show sensitivity.

Jody's Dad taught him to suppress emotion, and certainly not to show it publicly. His father, like many men of his era, many men of today for that matter, believed that males who showed emotion revealed weakness.

What this hard cold world needs is more boys and men who *are* sensitive. Men who aren't afraid of tears, their own or other peoples.

I'd like to see more men remove the macho mask of control and show the love and hurt and joy of being human that we all experience. I think if more adult males showed the little boys in their lives that real men do cry, as well as eat quiche, that this world would be the kinder and gentler place President Bush keeps talking about. And certainly it would be more comfortable for sensitive men like my son, Jody, who should, by all that's fair, have a world in which to laugh and cry and celebrate their 30th birthdays.

Play with Me

As a result of my son's death, I now appreciate my grandchildren so much more. I understand how precious their lives are, that they won't be little for long, and that I should enjoy the pre-school and after-school time as much as I can. It will not come again.

Even with this knowledge, it's easy to get caught up in our busy lives and say, "I don't have time to do that today," even though it's something that would give us much pleasure. Stressed out parents, pulled in so many different directions these days, suffer most from the "I don't have time right now, maybe later" syndrome.

I was caring for two of my grandchildren one day. I was writing in my office and they were playing in the kid's playroom nearby. The four year old wandered in, sat down, and for a few minutes quietly watched me work. Then without demanding or accusing, in almost an apologetic way, he said, "I guess you wouldn't have time to come and play with me, would you?"

I looked down into those soft brown eyes and remembered my son and the times I could have spent with him, but didn't because I was too busy. "You bet I'd have time to play," I said and I smiled as he did.

I can't remember spending a better afternoon.

I also suspect that it was time well invested in that child's future, and mine.

If we're always too busy for our children when they're young, should we be surprised that they haven't got time for us when we're old?

Love

Is there any such thing as loving all your children or grandchildren exactly the same? Equal portions of love and affection doled out in exact measurements? I don't think so. I don't think it's possible to love any two people the same. You could have a dozen children and love them all, in different ways and for different reasons. You love them for all those unique qualities that keep them from being the same. A woman with seven children who was named "Mother of the Year," was asked if she had any favorites. "Of course I do," came her soft reply. "Every mother does." Surprised at her answer, the interviewer asked which ones. The mother answered without hesitation, "It's the one who is sick, until he or she gets well, it's the one who is away from home, until they return, it's the one who seems to need my love the most at that particular time."

The squeaky wheel, the child in need, the child who asks for love and attention, usually does get the oil. And you know something, when a wheel is oiled it turns much more smoothly than the strong silent one that labors without oil. Some children reach out for love, they have open arms and hearts. They speak their needs and feelings. Other children hold back, waiting for you to come to them, to prove you care. Thus, unfortunately, the child that probably needs it most gets the least amount of love. Perhaps the answer is in oiling all the wheels in our life, squeaky or not. But even so each drop of oil will be dispensed differently because every wheel is different. They all make our world go around, but in different ways.

Stepchild — Love's Stumbling Block

Don't let anyone kid you, marrying someone with children is a lot harder than marriyng someone without.

I don't care who tells you otherwise, you *are not* that child's parent. Even if both the biological mother and father have given you, the stepparent, a position of authority, and this is rare, when hard decisions have to be made, and strong action taken, no one is going to take your say seriously, or allow you to have the deciding vote.

You'll be lucky if you're even included in the discussions concerning your stepchild, after all, it's *their* child.

Stepparenting is a lot of work, frustration, drained bank accounts, spoiled romantic weekends, and sexless vacations because you're all sleeping in the same room. *And,* if you expect to be thanked for your efforts and sacrifices you're living in the world of TV sitcoms.

I think stepparenting, more than anything else in life, has to be approached in the most altruistic way possible. What you do for your stepchild must be done because it's the right thing to do, and best for the child, and for no other reason. You shouldn't do it to make points with your spouse, or avoid trouble with his or her ex, or in hopes of developing a lasting relationship with this child, that might even endure as long as the ones he has with his real parents. That sometimes happens, but certainly shouldn't be the reason you spend time, energy, and a great deal of patience on this child.

The danger in this open, un-selfish approach to stepparenting is that you're going to grow to love this child who doesn't carry your genes, your name, and rarely carries out the garbage. There is no in-born sense of loyalty. Stepchildren do not come with an unquestioning guarantee to love you back, or even a feeling of obligation that they have to listen to you.

However, as a stepmother of many years, I'm extremely happy to be able to tell you that if expressions of love and gratitude do surface from a stepchild, you'll experience the joy of getting a precious gift you didn't expect.

Christopher, 20 years old at the time, who had been living away from home for six months, returned to live with his father and me. He had decided to go back to college, get a job, and to get more firmly established before going out on his own again. In his absence I had been wearing two good-looking sweaters that he left behind. His taste in clothing, and his ability to talk someone into buying him the best, greatly exceeds mine. On the first cold day of that fall I pulled out the sweaters and told him how much I had enjoyed wearing them the winter before. I asked what he had paid for them and offered to buy them from him. Christopher hadn't started his new job yet, and I knew he could use the money.

With an indignant look on his face my stepson said, "I wouldn't take any money from you. After all you've done for me, don't you even think about giving me any money. I'm glad I can give you *something*, I wish it was more."

He didn't realize it, but with those words, he had.

Pets are Like Children Too

Duski Dog stood about 18-inches tall, and that was when she was sitting up on her hind legs begging for food. When she wasn't doing that her well fed belly practically dragged on the ground. Duski's little legs couldn't have been more than a couple of inches long.

On the beach her stomach was always sandy, when it snowed you'd find icicles there. But oh how she loved both the beach and the snow. Whether she was running after sea gulls, or children on sleds, she never tired of the game of chase. And she could run faster than most dogs twice her size. She often beat the sleds to the bottom of the hill, and once, at the seashore, to our embarrassment, on a crowded beach she actually caught a sea gull. Boy, did we get stares of disapproval for letting our dog do such a thing, and she got named "Killer Dog."

Though I didn't know her heritage, I always thought that she must have been a cross between a dachshund and a scottish terrier. She was long and short like a dachshund, and she had the black wiry hair of a scotty. She had a boxy beard on her long nose, wild eyebrows, a long tail, and floppy ears that hung from the sides of her head like socks pinned to a clothesline. I thought she was beautiful, but when other people saw her for the first time they often smiled, broadly. Some even laughed out loud.

One thing on which we all agree was the love and intelligence that showed in her soft brown, knowing eyes. When Duski looked at you her gaze penetrated your soul; you felt sure she knew even your most private thoughts. Duski was a dog you talked to, in depth, because you felt sure that she understood every word you said.

Duski found *us*. It was during the summer of 1977, following my son's death, that she came to my back door at dusk; thus her name.

She was just a couple of months old. We checked around to see if she belonged to any of our neighbors, and were relieved to find out she didn't. We welcomed this adorable creature, this new life, with the gratefulness that one greets sunshine after a long period of rain. I willingly let her invade my heart and my life. I suppose the ache I carried from losing my son caused me to cling to the companionship of this dog.

I started taking Duski everywhere I went. If for some reason I couldn't take her with me I worried about leaving her home. I was afraid she'd be lonely, and think I didn't love her anymore. The simple truth was that I missed her when she wasn't with me. One summer, after Jack and I were married, we rented an apartment for a week, in Ocean City, were pets weren't allowed. I was so miserable without my dog that one morning, before dawn, Jack got up without telling me where he was going, drove the three hours back to Baltimore, returning after another three hours of driving, with Duski. I've never loved him more. When the owner of the apartment found out we had a dog in there we had to pay to have the place fumigated when we left, but it was worth it to have Duski with me for my vacation. The experience caused us to spend part of that week looking for a condo to buy so we could take Duski to the beach whenever we wanted. It was an expensive dog house but we *all* enjoyed it for years to come.

During the 13-years of Duski's life we shared some momentous times.

Duski watched as my daughter Marjorie went off to California, where she lived for several years. And when I went to California to visit, Duski went with me. I took Duski on planes, trains, boats, a San Francisco cable car, and into hotels and restaurants where she didn't belong.

As my daughter O'Donnell posed for her wedding pictures Duski gingerly stepped onto the long bridal train, of ivory lace, that had been carefully swirled around in front of my daughter's feet by the photographer. Duski sat motionless, facing the camera, ready to become part of the picture history of this special day in the life of our family. Unfortunately, the photographer didn't see Duski's intrusion as a great candid shot that would have meant more to us than all the other pictures he took that day, but rather a disruption of the formal portrait he had set out to get. He shooed Duski away before any of us could stop him.

Duski shared everything. The good times and the not-so-good. There was the courtship between Jack and me, made more difficult in the aftermath of the two suicides. Duski was there to listen, and to share the tears. One of the nice things about a devoted dog is that they do listen, but they don't make judgments, give advice, or take sides.

In 1979 when Jack and I were married, outside on the south lawn of my house, Duski sat by our feet as we said our vows. Six weeks after our marriage *Duski* had puppies. It seemed that our whole family was overdosing on love during that period of time.

On the day the puppies were born I had left Duski at home, when I went to work, because I knew she was due any day. I had also left her outside since it was summertime, and warm. However, when I arrived home that night, in the middle of a thunderstorm, Duski was no where to be found. I can remember frantically running around through the wind and rain, with lightning crackling nearby, screaming for Duski. I was pleading for her to forgive me for leaving her home alone and begging her to come out from wherever she was hiding. Finally I found her quietly curled up under the porch steps. She didn't make a sound and she didn't move, but there, in the flashlight beam were those eyes shining back at me.

"Oh, thank you dear God," I said out loud, expressing my relief. Then I began to scold Duski. (Why is it that when we're worried about someone, and then find out they're all right, we yell at them?) "You had me worried half sick. I'm sorry I left you outside alone, but why didn't you come when I called you?"

Before crawling under the steps to get Duski I yelled to Jack, who had also been looking for her, that I had found her. He came running. "I guess she doesn't want to come out in the rain," I said, as I crouched down to get under the steps. When I got close to her I realized that Duski wasn't afraid of getting wet, Duski was giving birth. One puppy had already been born.

Jack and I quickly got Duski and her puppy inside. We made a birthing bed out of towels and an old blanket, and then sat up with our dog as she delivered six more puppies. A night of near desperation became one of celebration and joy.

A week later our euphoria was dowsed with despair.

During another violent thunderstorm, lightning struck our house and set it ablaze. No one was home except Duski and her pups. We had left the back door ajar so that Duski could get in and out, never dreaming that the reason she'd need to get out would be to escape a fire.

As the flames engulfed the downstairs and the heat became intense Duski must have realized that she'd have to leave. She tried to get her puppies out, but the flames must have spread too quickly for her to complete the job. The firemen found two puppies outside, struggling to survive. A neighbor took them to the vet but they later died.

When I got home Duski was again not around.

But this time when she heard my voice calling her name she came running up out of the woods. I'm sure the flames and the sirens of the fire trucks had scared her into hiding. I picked up my little dog, held her tight and wept into her thick black coat that reeked of smoke. I cried for her pain, and mine.

That night Jack and Duski and I spent the night next door at my parent's house. It's the house that my daughter Marjorie has since inherited. Duski was restless, and all night long she kept going to the front door and scratching on it to get out. Finally, at dawn, I let her out. It was as if I had opened a starting gate. She raced across the lawn, through the garden, under the fence and around to the back of our burned out house. Barefoot I raced behind her trying to keep her in sight.

"Come back here Duski. Come back here. Don't go over there." She paid no attention to me. When I rounded the corner of the house, to my surprise, I saw Duski digging wildly in the dirt under a log near the back door. I stood behind her and watched, completely bewildered as to why she was doing this. I didn't have to wait long for the answer. In seconds, from this shallow bunker that served as protection against the heat and flames, Duski uncovered one of her puppies that she had hidden there. With her mouth, she reached down, gently picked up the tiny black puppy by the scruff of it's neck and carried it back to where I stood. I dropped to my knees to receive this whimpering little gift of life.

Through the tears of joy and amazement I talked to my dog. "Oh Duski you saved a puppy. How in the world did you know to do that?"

I brushed the dirt from the puppy's shiny black coat and reached over to stoke Duski with love and admiration.

But Duski was not yet ready to rest. Her work was not finished. With her live puppy safe in my lap Duski bounded up the back steps and into the charred ruins of the house. She dug through the rubble of the laundry room, which is where she last saw her puppies alive.

With each discovery of a puppy, one by one, she carried the lifeless bodies outside. With tears as my only solace, I watched quietly this incredible display of maternal instinct. When there were four charred little bodies by my side, and the one squirming, now whining puppy in my lap, I broke the silence with words spoken as gently as I knew how. "That's all of them Duski. The other two were taken to the vet." It wasn't my words that stopped her from going back into the house. She knew she had gotten two other puppies out, she just didn't know what had happened to them. She began sniffing around outside for clues as to where they might be. I knew that, dead or alive, Duski would need to see those other two puppies if she was to have any peace of mind, which is what we eventually did.

"Come on," I said, "let's go over to the other house. Let's show everyone the puppy you saved; besides she's hungry. You've got some mothering to do."

I picked Duski up and carried her, along with the puppy, over to my parent's house. I knew she didn't want to leave the others, and wasn't about to go on her own.

After Duski and "Blaze," the name we gave to the puppy, were settled down together, I went back and buried the remains of Duski's brood.

As for Duski and Blaze, they were never separated for as long as Duski lived, and I don't think Blaze ever forgot that Duski was her mother, or that Duski had saved her life.

Blaze grew to be a much larger dog than her mother but she never took advantage of Duski. She always showed respect. If there was only one bowl of food, Blaze would wait until her mother had finished eating. Blaze loved to eat, but not more than she loved Duski.

When Duski died during the summer of 1990 from kidney failure, Blaze grieved as hard as the rest of us.

Duski and Blaze each had a doggie bed in our bedroom. When Duski died and I removed Duski's bed Blaze didn't even want to come in the room. That night when Jack and I went to bed we coaxed Blaze into the bedroom, but she went in Jack's closet and just stared at the wall. Several days later when Blaze finally got back in her bed to sleep, she curled up facing away from where Duski's bed had been.

Duski is buried under the Japanese Black Pine out by the fish pond.

Blaze gets extra love these days, though I'm not sure I'll ever feel as close to any other animal as I did to Duski. However, there *is* this orange barn cat that recently wandered onto the farm. Blaze chases it, but I've been feeding the cat when Blaze isn't looking, and it's now coming up to the brick wall out near the barbecue grill. My grandchildren and I can watch him from the kitchen window. I've named him "Rusty Rover." The children just call him "The Barn Cat."

Who knows where this relationship will lead? Anyone who has developed a deep attachment for an animal realizes that pets are like children, and there's no predicting how far an investment of love and time will take you.

Out of the Mouths
of Grandchildren

Jack was having a conversation about pets with 5-year-old Jay. "I wish the barn cat would be more friendly," Jay was saying. "Then I'd have two cats to play with, the barn cat and my cat 'Panther.' Don't you wish the barn cat would come around more?" Jay asked.

"No, not really," said Jack, who is allergic to cat hair.

"Why? Don't you like cats?" Jay continued questioning this lack of enthusiasm for an animal he though was pretty neat.

"Not really," Jack admitted reluctantly, not wanting to discourage Jay's appreciation of cats. "I just like dogs more."

"Why?"

"Well," Jack began, "Cats are very independent; for one thing, they don't come when they're called. Does your cat, Panther, come when he's called?"

"Yeah," Jay said strongly, defending the feline species and trying to convince Jack that he was wrong about cats as pets.

"He always comes when I call him."

"Always?" Jack asked skeptically.

"Yeah, Panther always comes when I call him." Jay paused a moment to ponder if he was being completely honest and then added, "except on Mondays. Panther never comes when he's called on Mondays."

5 Forever Someone's Child

*Our parents might die but
we'll always be their child.*

Role Reversal

My father died August 24, 1988. My mother died two years and two days before that. I somehow thought that once I got over the initial grief of their death that I'd simply go on with my life without looking back, or wishing that they were still around to be a part of that life. But I've discovered that it doesn't work that way. I find myself saying things like, "I wish Daddy had lived to see his great granddaughter ride her pony." He loved horses and riding with such a passion he would have been thrilled to see what an accomplished rider she is becoming. And often when I'm gardening and I notice a particularly pretty flower, I think, "Wouldn't mother have enjoyed seeing that." I want to cut it and take it to her, as I did when she was alive.

With the passage of time the stress and trauma of my parents' deaths, and in my father's case, the months leading up to that death, have faded, and now the memories of their elder years, like old photographs, bring more joy than pain, and the wish that we could have had more time together.

In the summer of 1986 my father suffered a major stroke that affected him mentally as well as physically. He was 82 at the time, still practicing dentistry, maintaining a heavy patient schedule, with an eight and sometimes ten hour work day. My mother, 81, was his secretary/receptionist, and worked the same schedule.

My father's stroke ended a life of tenacious independence. He not only had control of his own existence, he also believed he knew what was best for everyone else. Over the years he doled out advice and opinions to his patients, as well as to his family. When I was a young woman, my father's self-importance annoyed me.

As I matured I learned to ignore it, preferring to focus on, what I considered, his more admirable characteristics; generosity, kindness, and his determination and diligence in whatever he did.

When his assertiveness was destroyed by the stroke, never to re-surface again, I found I missed it terribly. I longed to hear him tell me, just one more time, how much harder he worked when he was my age, and how over-paid I was just for going on television.

The first few days after his stroke my father couldn't even feed himself. I spent those days either crying, or when I was with him or my mother, trying to suppress my tears. It was a torturous thing to see someone so strong, someone I had leaned on for most of my life, not even to be able to defend himself against the many indignities that hospitals and health care providers often impose upon the elderly who have become helpless.

I remember walking down the hospital corridor early one morning on my way to see my father, and hearing his loud moans long before I entered his room.

He was tied in bed; strapped in place by something the nurses called a "Posey." A straight-jacket is what it was. It's put on the patient then tied under the bed so that the person can't move at all. He was flat on his back, the most uncomfortable position for my Dad, because of a chronically bad back.

His feet were tied to the bottom of the bed, and he literally could not move an inch in any direction. If someone did this to a prison inmate, or a prisoner-of-war, it would be considered a crime against their human rights.

I ripped away at the bonds holding my father, trying to calm him with my voice as I worked with my hands, first freeing his legs, and then the rest of his body.

"It's okay Daddy, I'm here now. It's Susie, You'll be free in a minute, and I promise you no one will do this to you *ever* again."

Once untied, my father rolled quickly onto his left side. He curled up his legs and slid his hands under the pillow that was holding his head. He let out a huge sigh of relief.

The stroke had caused some temporary dementia, some mental confusion, and often my father didn't know where he was, or recognize familiar people. However, he always knew me and called me by name. When no one else could get him to cooperate, I'd simply tell him what to do and he'd do it without hesitation or question, like an obedient child.

On that day, lying in that hospital bed, curled up in a fetal position, exhausted from a night of pain, fear and no sleep, he opened his eyes and in a child-like way he said, "I'm glad you're here, Susie. The people here aren't very nice. I don't want to come here on vacation anymore."

"We won't bring you here on vacation anymore," I said, smiling to reassure him. He closed his eyes, and like a baby feeling satisfied and secure, he drifted into a deep sleep.

When I was sure he was asleep, and would be safe, I stormed out of the room and down the hall to the nurses' station. Without asking who was responsible for tying my father to the bed, or who was in charge, I began my tirade.

"I don't ever, ever want my father tied up again. I wouldn't do that to a dog and you're not going to do it to my father." I was determined not to cry, but my emotions overrode my intentions. Having lost control of the tears I no longer tried to temper my words. Fueled by anger at a system that would advocate such inhumane treatment, I began making threats.

"Furthermore, if it ever happens again I promise you that someone's job will be in jeopardy."

One of the nurses who seemed completely unmoved, even indifferent to my anger, emotion, and threats, coolly recited the hospital policy. "When we restrain a patient it is always for that patient's own good. Your father could have hurt himself if he fell out of bed. He is confused and we were protecting him from any harm he might have caused himself."

I wasn't buying this rationale.

"You tie patients so you don't have to be bothered with them, and you *will not* tie my father again. Do you understand?" I shouted. The angrier I got the more controlled that nurse became. Her air of superiority was getting the best of me. She spoke calmly and quietly.

"We have a lot of patients to care for. We can't give your father round the clock personal attention. If that's what you want, you need to hire private nurses."

"That's what I want. So who do I see about hiring private nurses?" I asked.

"We'll send the social worker around to your father's room to talk to you."

I started to walk away then turned back for one last shot. "You should have told me about the private nurses when they brought my father down from intensive care, before this happened."

I returned to my father's room, beginning to feel guilty that I had lost control. I could have accomplished the same thing without getting so upset. And then I thought, "what if we couldn't afford private nurses, and what about the people who can't?" I felt less guilty.

I sat down next to the bed and looked at my father's handsome face. He continued to sleep soundly. At 82 he still had a full head of silky white hair. His mustache was trimmed neatly as I had always known it to be. "A man of dignity," I thought, "in such an undignified predicament."

Although feeling a little guilty, and somewhat ashamed that I had made such a scene at the nurses' station, sitting there looking at my Dad, I thought: "He would have done the same for me, in fact he did do just about the same thing when I was a child."

It was the night before my sixth birthday, a hot August evening. For the first, and last, time in my life I developed a severe Asthma attack. It was about nine o'clock.

I was in bed, and my father was out in the barn, grooming one of his thoroughbred horses. The windows in my room were open, and he heard me gasping for breath. He and my mother arrived at my bedside about the same time. Not only was I struggling to breathe, I had turned blue from lack of oxygen.

The story I later heard was that when he called the doctor and asked him to come to the house right away to see me, the doctor had said, "give her an aspirin, and let's see how she is in the morning."

It was not a common practice for people to go to hospitals on their own then. They waited to be referred by the family physician. Most hospitals didn't even have "Emergency Rooms" forty-five years ago. That night my father said to the doctor, "If this child dies tonight you will have me to deal with, and your life won't be worth a hill of beans."

My father would never have physically harmed that doctor but the threat brought him to our house that night and his visit saved my life.

As I thought about that incident the guilt I had been feeling, about yelling at those nurses, disappeared.

In two weeks my father had recovered sufficiently to return home. I helped him out of the car, and as we walked slowly up the front walk to his house, my mother opened the door to welcome her husband home.

"I'll bet you never expected to see me *walk* back into this house did you sweetie pie?" my father said, smiling at this woman who *had been* preparing herself to face her husband's death.

Tears of gratitude and joy filled the deep wrinkles at the corners of her eyes. She was unable to speak.

A week later my mother died, quietly, in her sleep from heart failure.

My father was devastated. He started to wish he had not survived the stroke and that he and mother could have gone together. He truly felt that he had nothing to live for. In such a short period of time, three weeks, he had lost his health, his dental practice, and contact with his patients who were his friends, and now, the only woman he had ever loved, his wife of 53 years.

On the day mother died, my father, sobbing like a lost child, looked at me and choked out the words, "At least I still have you." I knew I could never make my father really happy again, but on that day I made two promises, one to him and one to myself. I promised him that, according to his wishes, he would never see the inside of a nursing home. I told him that he could be assured that he would live out the rest of his days in his home no matter what it took and that when the time came he would die at home, just as mother had.

Being put in a nursing home had been a long time fear of my father's. Daddy had been haunted by the experience he had gone through with his own father. When my grandfather had a stroke, and could no longer afford to stay in his home, he came to our house. It was an emotional as well as physical strain on my mother.

She was a woman who always put the needs of others before her own. But caring for my bed-ridden grandfather, shopping and preparing meals, transporting nurses back and forth to the house to be there when she couldn't, and all the rest that goes with taking care of someone who can't do for himself, wore her down.

My brother and I were teenagers at the time, adding the burden and problems of adolescence to her life. The combination was too much. And when my father realized the toll it was taking on my mother he felt he had no choice but to put his dad in a nursing home. However, my father vowed then not to let that happen to him, if he could help it.

He started putting money aside; investing it for his old age. He wanted to remain independent, and he wasn't going to rely on insurance, or his children, or social security to make that happen. It was only because of his foresight and savings that I was able to keep my promise to my Dad, and keep him in his home.

I could never have afforded to do it on my own. During the two years he lived after his stroke, it took most of the money he had saved to pay for the full time help needed to care for him.

Had he lived longer, and the money run out, I would have brought him into my home. If it would have been impossible for me to care for him — well, as he was with his father, and so many others are, I'd have been faced with breaking my promise and looking for the best nursing home I could find. There are good ones, it's just that even good nursing homes remove the person from daily contact with their family.

With Daddy in his own home, nearby, I saw him twice every day, sometimes more. He attended the birthday parties, the family celebrations of all holidays, the christenings of two of his great-grandchildren. He was still very much a part of his family.

We often held the celebrations at his house so it would be convenient for him, and he would still feel like the center of things. I think it was the best possible existence for an elderly person, like him, who was no longer healthy and capable of living on his own.

But, it was only possible because my father, when he was fifty, thought about the future and what he might face and what he would need to live out his years exactly as he wanted.

Have I done the same thing? No, but I'm beginning to realize that I need to begin — NOW, that I'm 50.

The promise I made to *myself* back then was that I'd make *extra* time for my Dad. This was to be his time, but as it turned out, it was mine as well. I told myself that, after he died, I didn't want to look back and say, "I wish I had spent more time with my father when I had the chance. I wish we had done more things together. I wish we had talked and that I had recorded some of his stories to re-play when he was gone."

In the two years and two days that he survived my mother I did everything I thought I should do, and all the things I thought I would like to do; and now, I look back with no regrets and a lot of fond memories.

I got to know another side of my father; a more mellow man. Out from under the pressures of earning a living, maintaining a farm, raising children, and all the rest that kept him so busy, I got to see the poet, philosopher, and easy-going individual who had been suppressed so much of his life by that hardworking man bent on "success."

Sometimes my dad and I would just sit by the fireside. Sometimes we went for a ride in my Jeep around the farm, his property, that he so dearly loved and could no longer work on or walk around. Often we'd go for a drive around the countryside. Once we drove into Baltimore city and through the neighborhood where he grew up.

On tape, I started recording stories about his life as he remembered it. He remembered it all, to the tiniest detail. I asked about his first childhood memory; the first recollection of his life. I thought it would be about his family, his mother and father, or one of his four siblings. He had three brothers with whom he was extremely close, and one older sister.

But instead he began to tell me about one of his early childhood playmates.

From the tape recording I made, my father's voice comes back to me, gravelly with age, and filled with pain.

"The first thing I remember from my childhood — I was about four I guess — my mother had bought me a new set of reins to play horse and driver. I couldn't wait to drive the boy next door. We put the reins on him, and started up the street. There was a streetcar that came up that street. It was the other side of Mount Street, on Baker Street. Just as this boy and I went to cross the street, this streetcar came along.

The motorman was banging on the bell as hard as he could. All I knew was if I let my friend pull me forward any further I'd be run over, and if I pulled back on the reins there was a chance he'd be run over. I pulled back and he fell down in front of the streetcar. And the streetcar ran over him. I was so scared. I ran home and all I told my mother was that my new horse reins had been cut in half by the streetcar.

There was quite a commotion and I had to go to police court, and when I did all I did was cry. I couldn't tell anyone what happened. I was sorry I couldn't tell them exactly what happened — I was too afraid. That was my first fear in life. I knew I should say, 'look, I pulled him back,' but I didn't. I couldn't say I caused my friend to be killed."

For all those years my father carried the guilt for causing the death of his friend. I think I was the first person to hear that story, and the truth that had been locked away for almost eighty years. I like to think telling me about the tragedy that had touched his life as a 4-year-old boy, brought him some peace in his final days.

There were many stories and thoughts my father shared with me on tape. Things he felt he no longer needed to keep secret. He revealed his belief that his mother had never been "in love" with his father. He said that she loved an actor she had met at Ford's Theater in Baltimore. He felt she married his father for security.

There is so much history, romance, intrigue, adventure, and wisdom on the tapes, all of which I might not have known or shared if I hadn't made those recordings. I'll cherish them for as long as I live, and I will certainly pass them on to my grandchildren so that they can remember great-granddaddy, hear his voice, and hear him talk about their family of generations past, and a different way of life.

When I promised myself to make time for my father I thought I was doing it for him, but I now realize, quite clearly, that I was the beneficiary.

I remember taking him to the last "Maryland Hunt Cup" horse race he would ever see. It was the last Saturday in April of 1988.

The Maryland Hunt Cup, which is traditionally held the last Saturday in April, is considered the world's most difficult cross-country jumping race. Even more of a challenge than the English "Grand National," because the jumps are higher and made of post and rail or board fences.

The Grand National has many "brush" jumps, which the horses don't have to clear completely to get over. The horses can brush through without being toppled. When a horse's legs hit the solid, unyielding fences of the Hunt Cup, the horse usually falls or is knocked off balance so badly that it unseats the rider.

The Hunt Cup is a great sporting event, but for me, it's much more than that. It's one of the first recollections I have as a child. My mother and father would take my brother and me out to the beautiful Worthington Valley, where the race is held on private land.

Joining thousand of other people, we'd park the car in a field and then walk to the hillside over-looking the race course. We'd walk through tall, lush pastureland dotted with buttercups and a few dandelions, very few. Those fields were much too well cared for to spout many weeds of any kind.

My mother and father, dressed in tweed suits and "sensible" shoes, would lead us through the soggy bottom land, and across a stream, before we started the long climb up the steep hill. Once on the hillside we'd find just the right spot to spread out a blanket for our picnic lunch, which included, for the adults, mint juleps, drunk from silver cups.

Later we'd run down to the paddock to see the horses before the race; my parents stopping along the way to chat with friends, some of whom they only saw once a year at this race.

We never missed the Maryland Hunt Cup no matter what the weather. I can remember standing along side my father on a rainy, dismal day staring into the fog trying to watch the horses run the course. My father was holding binoculars up to his eyes. "What do you see, Daddy? What do you see?" I asked excitedly, wondering who was winning.

"I don't see a damn thing," he said disgustedly. "It's like trying to watch a horse race through pea soup."

But, there we were standing in the rain, dutifully looking in the direction of the race and watching nothing more than thick fog moving across the valley.

And so it was, with that background of family tradition, that I took my father to see his last Hunt Cup.

April 30, 1988 was a glorious day, warm and sunny with just enough clouds to make it picture perfect.

I was having breakfast with Daddy in his dining room. The sun was almost too warm coming through the large bay window.

My father's head was bent low over his plate as he ate. His thin arms rested on the edge of the table. He still wore a heavy winter robe to warm his frail body.

"How would you like to go to the Hunt Cup this afternoon?" I asked. His head jerked back, his eyes became bright with interest. A smile replaced the lifeless look that I was seeing much too often those days.

"Is today the last Saturday in April?" he questioned.

I smiled as I nodded, thinking, "There's nothing wrong with his mind."

"It sure is the last Saturday in April. You want to go?"

His expression turned sad as he looked back down at his plate.

"Oh, I don't know, Susie. I couldn't walk up that hill you know." I wanted to cry.

"We won't walk up the hill. Let's just drive over there this afternoon and see what's going on. What do you say?"

"Okay," he said with renewed interest, "But first I'm going back to bed to take a nap."

A public road runs through the middle of the Hunt Cup race course, so what I did that afternoon was to drive along that road where my father could see the action; the people walking up the hill, the horses parading to the start.

The race course crosses the road in two places. They put sawdust on top of the macadam at those spots for the horses to run over. I drove back and forth on that road, timing it perfectly, so that when the race was about to start my car was stopped by one of the state troopers assigned to control traffic during the race. I had to pull over to the side of the road and stay there until the race was over. I was stuck right where I wanted to be, in the middle of the race course. Since the horses ran right past us, my father could see it all, better than he ever had before, without getting out of the car.

I have many such wonderful memories from the two and a half years I spent as my father's guardian.

It often doesn't seem right when a child is put in the position of controlling the life of a parent, even when that child is middle-aged and the parent is elderly. It can be a very uncomfortable, worrisome situation for both, and certainly one with many time-consuming burdens for the caretaker. But there are many blessings as well and I now find myself wishing I had created the same kind of time with my mother that I was forced to experience with my dad.

I certainly don't wish my mom had lost her health or independence. She died exactly as she always hoped she would, as I hope I will, in her home, at 82, never forced to be dependent on anyone. She still drove, took care of her house, enjoyed her family, had a large circle of friends; a good life. But her sudden death, and then what I shared with my father, makes me realize, once more, that we shouldn't put off doing things, for someone else, or for ourselves.

We need to establish priorities, make plans and commitments, and enjoy the people we love while we have them with us. My experience with my father taught me, that if we do, there are far fewer regrets.

Daddy's Little Girl — Mother's Daughter

I was Daddy's little girl. I looked like him, everybody said I did, and I wanted to look like him.

I had inherited his hazel eyes. My mother had blue eyes.

My face was square like my Dad's. My mother's face was round.

Daddy taught me to ride horses; to swim; ice skate; ski; to play ball, and even to go hunting.

My mother taught me to be polite; to fix my hair; to get dressed up in pretty clothes. She taught me to get to school on time, and to do my homework, so I'd have time to do what I really wanted to do, when my father got home, to ride horses, play ball, go swimming, and all the things I enjoyed doing with my Dad.

My father was my pal and I was his friend and play-mate.

When Daddy had to work, Mother was there to meet the bus after school.

She took me shopping with her.

She took me to church.

She took me to the Red Cross when she volunteered, and gave blood.

She dragged me along when she visited the sick and elderly.

I couldn't wait to get home to be with my Dad.

He'd come home, on a summer night, pick me up and swing me high in the air. "Okay, Shrimp, what are we going to do this evening?"

He'd kiddingly call me Shrimp because I was tall for my age. I was tall, just like my Dad.

Along about the time boys came into my life something happened to my relationship with my father. I was no longer Daddy's little girl. Something had changed, my Dad stepped aside, and the closeness was gone.

I was still my mother's daughter, but I no longer seemed to have much in common with my Dad.

I wish we had found a way to stay close. I wish we had found a way to communicate as well as we had played games.

It wasn't until he was old that we rediscovered each other, and how much we enjoyed being together.

And it was he who said to me, one day after my mother had died, and I was caring for him, "You're so much like your mother. You even look like her now."

My eyes filled with tears. Daddy's girl had grown up to be just like her mother.

And now, nothing pleases me more.

Mother's Day Tribute To My Mom — Elizabeth Miller Scheid

In thinking about how to describe my mother that would help you understand how wonderful she was, it dawned on me that it was all the things she didn't do that made her a saint among the holy sisterhood of all mothers.

She never raised her voice. My mother never yelled at me. When this soft spoken, gentle woman got serious, when her eyes grew sad, you knew that you needed to listen and do whatever she said to make her smile again.

My mother never criticized me; I heard only praise and encouragement from her.

My mother never compared me to anyone else.

She never said that I should be more like someone else, but she also never said that I was better than other people. However, her praise led me to believe that she thought I was pretty special, which raised my feelings of self-worth.

My mother never said don't, she always said, do. Instead of saying "Don't you dare go across the street alone," she said, "Stay on this side of the street where it's safe unless an adult is with you."

My mother never said can't, only can. Never "You can't do that." What I heard was, "You can do anything you put your mind and energy into."

My mother never said I was wrong, and that I had made a mess of things. She let me figure that out for myself and when I did she was there with support to help me right the wrong, or to offer nonjudgemental comfort when the mistake was irreversible.

My mother never asked for or demanded love and attention, she only knew how to give it. And, as she grew old, my mother remained as independent as possible, never asking for help but grateful when it was given. My mother was never a burden, only a blessing.

My mother didn't give me the world, but she gave me what I needed to make a place for myself in the world. She gave me the tools to carve out a life that is richer and more secure because of all the things she didn't do.

Volunteers

My mother gave of herself, to her family, and to the community. She showed me, by her example, that it's important to be a volunteer. I have since experienced the benefits, for myself, of giving of one's time and talents; of giving back.

Can you imagine what life would be like in this country, in your community, without volunteers? It would be awful if all the hundreds and thousands of people who give of their time in service to organizations, hospitals, and individual needs, suddenly stopped doing that. I hate to think about life without those volunteers; who work in schools and daycare centers, in nursing homes and churches, the charities and the causes that change the way we view the world.

As an 88-year-old volunteer I met recently said, "Never underestimate the power or value of a volunteer."

But, for all the good works volunteers do, I think one of the most beneficial side affects, of volunteering, is the self-improvement the volunteer experiences. Put simply, people who volunteer are better human beings because of it. When people give of themselves they feel a sense of worth and importance. They realize that they can help improve the lives of others.

I first experienced this in my early twenties. Though my mother had set the example for me it was my first husband's Aunt Ada who got me involved as a volunteer. Coming from a generation and social standing where few women worked, in or out of the home, Aunt Ada believed that the proper thing for every proper young woman to do was to begin a volunteer job that would continue and mature as she did. Aunt Ada's mother, my first husband's grandmother, was a hospital volunteer well into her nineties.

Aunt Ada literally took me by the hand, drove me to the hospital where she and her mother were volunteers, and signed me up. It was decided that I would volunteer once a week as a play-lady in the pediatric unit.

At the time, this seemed really rather silly to me. I had to hire a baby-sitter to take care of my three small children at home so that I could go to the hospital and help take care of other people's children, for no pay. This "good work" was not only costing me time, but money as well.

I was young and self-centered and hadn't yet experienced the positive effects of being a volunteer. It didn't take long for that to happen.

On my second visit to the pediatric unit I noticed a child lying in a bed, back in the corner. He hadn't been there the week before. This child was almost completely wrapped in bandages. All I could see were his eyes. They peered out at me from the two open circles in his sterile encasement.

The sadness I saw in those eyes pulled me in his direction. As I neared his bedside the stench of burned flesh hit me with the nauseating reality of what had happened to him. Swallowing to suppress the urge to vomit, I opened my mouth to breath, and smiled at the child, hoping he hadn't noticed that the smell of his body was making me sick. I didn't want to turn away and make the boy feel that he was so repulsive that no one would want to be near him. There, in the hospital, it was the awful smell, later it would be the scars that would turn people away. I pulled a chair next to his bed, sat down, and carefully touched his bandaged hand.

Robby was seven years old. He had been burned in a house fire. Firemen had rescued him in an upstairs bedroom. They hadn't been able to save his mother and baby sister. His father and older brother escaped uninjured.

Robby's recovery was long and extremely difficult. As the weeks became months I found myself looking forward to my weekly volunteer visit to the hospital. I started bringing books, toys and games from home; things that my children loved, and I hoped he might also. I told him about my children and the farm and all the animals.

He loved hearing about them and I loved being able to take his mind off his physical pain and the grief he was experiencing over the death of his mother and sister.

After Robby got well enough to leave the hospital, though happy for him, I found myself missing him. On my first volunteer day following his departure, a kind and sensitive nurse could see I felt abandoned, that I was holding back with the other children, questioning the good sense of allowing an emotional involvement with a patient, knowing that the relationship would always eventually end.

She took me aside to tell me that the time I had spent with Robby had meant much more to him than a weekly diversion from the hospital routine. She said that it had also been medically beneficial. She told me that my visits had aided him in healing; had helped him want to get well. She said that during the early days of treatment, when the pain was so great, looking forward to those Wednesdays, when I'd be there, had helped him hold onto life. She said, "One day we were giving him a bath. It's an agonizing process, but one we have to do. He was crying and screaming. At one point he yelled out, as loud as he could, "I can't stand this anymore. I hate you. I hate you." After a while he stopped yelling and started sobbing, almost choking on his words, he said, "But the play-lady will be here tomorrow and that will be fun."

My experience with Robby helped me begin to understand my real value as a human being. That it doesn't matter who I am, how rich or poor; what my education, or background, I have the power to make a positive difference in another person's life. You don't have to be a volunteer to do this, but often good deeds are more effective when there are no financial rewards involved.

A nurse could have done what I did for Robby but he would have seen that as part of her job. As a volunteer I sent the message to that child that he must be pretty special; that his life must be valuable. After all the play-lady kept coming back to spend time with him. She didn't have to be there. She wasn't being paid, and he wasn't her child.

For whatever reason Aunt Ada knew what she was doing. Unfortunately not everyone has an Aunt Ada who will see to it that they become a volunteer.

If I had my way, every high school student would be asked to do community service before graduation, so that they, as teenagers, could experience the personal growth that comes from giving to other people. So that they might begin to realize the importance of life, theirs, as well as someone else's.

Self-esteem, self-confidence, self-worth goes up when selfless acts are performed.

Volunteers do good work, feel good about themselves, and want to do more. It's this benevolent chain of volunteers that has helped make this country live up to its ideals. And expanding this chain will help make each of us, and our community, stronger. President Bush calls volunteers "points of light." I think he's right. They sure do brighten the dark times.

Self-Esteem

One of the volunteer jobs I took on recently was to chair the Maryland Governor's Task Force on Self-Esteem. I considered the request quite seriously before taking on that added responsibility in my life, because I knew that volunteer job would be demanding, and it certainly was. But I also know that it was very worthwhile and extremely important.

California was the first to have a task force on self-esteem. Many people, including Gary Trudeau in his Doonesbury comic strip, found the idea of such a task force good grist for the joke mill. It was called the "touchy feely task force," "the ego or image committee," and some said, "you can't legislate self-esteem." Oh how I wish you could. That would make such a job much easier. No you can't impose self-esteem by law. But we can help one another find ways to improve the kind of self-respect and self-esteem that motivates us to be constructive rather than destructive. The results can be life saving, as well as money saving for taxpayers.

Think about it. When we feel good about who we are and what we can do, we don't commit suicide or allow our lives to be wasted by drugs. Anyone who respects the importance of all life won't cheat, rob or physically harm other people. With self-esteem we don't abuse people or allow them to abuse us. If we respect our minds and bodies, we don't misuse them or let them go to waste. We want to make something of ourselves.

I think by helping the caretakers of our communities, from parents and teachers to welfare workers and juvenile authorities, find ways of raising the levels of self-esteem among all our citizens, it is possible to reduce the welfare rolls, the prison population, the number of unwed mothers and high school drop-outs and, yes, the number of youth suicides.

Self-esteem, like love, is not easy to define. You know when you have it and when you don't, but it's hard to put it into words. The dictionary isn't much help. In trying to find a definition for my own use and understanding I came up with the following:

Self-Esteem . . . Understanding our value as a human being. Recognizing our own worth in spite of any physical, mental, emotional or economic limitations. Striving to live up to or exceed our acknowledged potential — and wanting to help others do the same. Believing that we can make a difference in the lives of the people around us.

However you define self-esteem, people in many walks of life are beginning to embrace the idea that helping people to understand themselves and feel good about who they are and what they can do, can make a positive difference in the quality of life for all of us.

Self-esteem will be the buzz word of the '90s. There will be self-esteem conferences and seminars. Books and papers will be written about this powerful and very personal thing. What excites me is what this means for individuals all across our country. Children, and the elderly; people on the job and family members. It's a return to the most powerful force we've ever known; the power of the individual.

How we use our talents:

How we treat other people:

How we relate to the needs of others; not just by giving our money but by giving our time.

How we conduct ourselves in every phase of life today determines how the next generation will live.

Negative influences often bring destructive action. When we dislike ourselves and others the result is often abuse and racism; murder and suicide; war, greed, and self-seeking success.

Each life we touch in a *positive* way has the potential to pass *that* along.

I'm encouraged by what I see happening with the self-esteem movement.

The kindergarten teacher of one of my grandchildren held a parents meeting to ask for volunteers.

She said, "I'm not looking for volunteers to run off copies of school work, to clean the classroom or to hold fund raisers. I want you to come and spend time in class with your child and the other children. I want you to read to them; to help with their art work; to encourage them in class. It's more important that they know that you're interested in them and what they do here than in working for the school."

She went on to say, "There will be no failures in this kindergarten class."

On a personal level, I have experienced the power of self-esteem, and the awful pain of its absence.

I don't think I could have accomplished what I have in my life if my parents hadn't instilled in me a feeling of self-worth, by encouraging me and telling me that I could do anything I set out to do.

When I said I wanted to be a TV reporter they didn't say, "Oh you can't do that, you don't have the necessary education." Instead they said, "Go for it. How can we help?"

When I said I felt I needed to write a book they didn't say, "You can't write a book. You don't have any training to write a book." They said, "Do it. Is there anything we can do to help?"

On the other side of the self-esteem issue, low or no self-esteem can be life threatening. I suffered the tragedy that resulted when my son's self-esteem plummeted. As a little boy he felt good about himself. I praised everything he did. He was self-confident and outgoing, and he was a success at everything he did.

But from age ten to seventeen a series of events changed all that. After years of struggling to hold onto a bad marriage, his father and I divorced. Eventually his father committed suicide. I had a demanding career and began a relationship with another man.

My son who had become shy and uneasy in social situations was expelled from the private boys school he had been attending, for a rules infraction, and had to transfer to a large public school where he knew no one. His sisters, with whom he was close, were away at college. And then his girl friend, his first romance, the one person to whom he was still clinging for security, broke up with him. Feeling inadequate, unneeded, and unimportant, he, too, took his life.

Tragically, I didn't see where my son's life was headed. I didn't understand at the time how devastating these events can be on a young person. And I didn't know that low self-esteem can be fatal.

I know now, and I'm encouraged by all the other people who are also becoming aware of the importance of self-esteem.

I see the self-esteem movement as a positive light in our future. The dawning of a brighter tomorrow, not only for us as individuals, but for our country.

6 Seasons and Off-seasons

I've come to look forward to the
expected, laugh at the unexpected,
and shake my fist at the jerks.

The Wonders of Winter

There's a lot not to like about winter: snarled traffic, high heating bills, or worse, downed power lines that leave you freezing cold. But I've grown to love winter and now think that there is much more to enjoy than to dislike.

I live in the country, and winter beyond the beltway is a most invigorating and often breathtakingly beautiful existence. It is also warm and cozy when you're by an open fire with a cup of hot chocolate or mulled cider, after a day of sledding or ice skating.

I love to sit by a window and watch the green pines turn a sugary white, or watch the sunrise over the newly placed coverlet of snow. The world is so quiet that even breathing seems like an intrusion.

Then, when the sun is well up above the horizon the world becomes one of energized life. Birds flitter around the bird feeders. Children laugh and speak words of wonder as they break through the unmarked snow and get the sleds out.

A child's voice calls up to my office window, where I'm supposed to be working. Instead, my nose is pressed against the frosted glass.

"When you're finished working MeMe will you come out to play?" the excited voice calls out.

"I'll get my snow clothes on," I yell back.

All of a sudden the work can wait a little longer, until another day.

I've come to feel that the cliché about not putting off till tomorrow what you can do today, should apply to your family as much, or more than to your work.

We play until the sun sets, watching as the snow turns to crystals of gold.

The nights are cold, but hearts are warm after a day like that. When you crawl between the flannel sheets, and the lights go out, the moon, reflecting off of the snow makes it almost too bright and beautiful to sleep.

But sleep you do, and well, for the day has been spent in perfect harmony with that which we can't control and that which we can.

Ski Trip

Before you start thinking that playing in the snow is always a worthwhile experience, let me tell you about a ski trip with my grandchildren.

Most people wouldn't even consider taking five children, ranging in age from two to six, to a ski slope for the day. Most people have better sense than that. Not me, not super-grandmom.

I not only took five of my six grandchildren to a ski resort, I did it during the busiest ski week of the year, between Christmas and New Year's. It seemed reasonable and even sane, before I left home.

I had reserved an instructor for the four older children. The 2-year-old was going to play happily in the child care center. I was going to ski the slopes, carefree, and with the satisfaction of knowing that I was providing my grandchildren with an early introduction to the sport of skiing. After all, isn't that what we grandmothers are for, to provide advantages for our grandchildren that we couldn't afford, or didn't have the time, to give our children?

To try and summarize a very long day, I knew I was in trouble when I pulled up to the curb outside the kid's ski center, and started to unload the five children and all their gear, and a man, directing traffic, shouted at me from about a half a block away.

"Move that car, now!" he said as he started walking toward me. "You can't park there."

"I'm not parking, I'm unloading. I have these five little children and all their ski stuff," I started to explain.

"Look, lady," said this unfriendly fellow, "everyone has ski stuff, this is a ski resort. And everyone coming here today has kids. Move the car."

I moved the car and we lugged the stuff about half a mile. Once inside the crowded kid's center the children waited, and not patiently, for two hours — *two hours!* — for the instructor I had booked a week earlier. When I questioned why, I was told that they were very busy, and I'd have to wait my turn. There was no apology and no explanation as to why a week ago I was told that an instructor would be available at nine a.m., and now he couldn't make it until eleven a.m.

Next, 2-year-old Tommy didn't take to the day care. I heard his screams from *outside* the building. When I went to rescue him I found him unattended, in fact the woman on duty didn't even know his name. And she tried to throw me out of the day care area saying, "Unidentified and un-authorized adults are not allowed back here."

"I'm this child's grandmother."

"How do I know that?" she shouted.

"You don't," I said, exasperated at the whole situation, "because you don't even know who this child is."

"Step back on the other side of that counter right now until I find out who you are," she said in a threatening way.

"I just told you who I am," I said, as I picked up Tommy to stop his crying.

Finally, the woman who checked Tommy in returned and acknowledged that I had been the one who had brought him there. And you can bet I was the one who got him out of there as quickly as I could.

Needless to say, I never took my skis off the top of my car. Instead of skiing, little Tommy and I spent most of the day watching his brother and cousins take turns being dragged up the hill by the rope tow.

At one point Tommy decided he was hungry. So I said, "Fine, lets go into the lodge and get something to eat." I wasn't helping the other kids to stand upright by staring at them and shaking my head, anyway. So Tommy and I trudged into the lodge, peeling off several layers of ski clothes as we went. When we got up the stairs and into the cafeteria we found a food line ten times longer than the lift line; at least a thirty minute wait. "Forget that," I said out loud. "We're not going to get in that mess."

"But I'm hungry, MeMe," whined Tommy. Just in time to avoid a scene I spied smoke drifting past the window from an outside fire. I looked out of the window and saw a grill with hot dogs and hamburgers, and no line.

"Come on Tommy, we're going to eat outside. Won't that be fun?"

"Yeah, MeMe, that'll be fun." Tommy was born a party animal. Suggest anything different, or merely mention the word fun, and his eyes light up. My spirits were lifting now, too. I quickly re-bundled Tommy, and re-dressed myself, and out we went, hurrying before others discovered this oasis. Once outside we headed for the smell of charcoal.

There were six workers behind the grill, all with their backs to Tommy and me. They were talking among themselves, ignoring the activity going on around them.

"Excuse me," I said politely.

No response.

"Excuse me," I said a little louder. "Could my grandson and I have a hot dog?" I asked.

One of the men turned around, and in a gruff, unpleasant voice, he said, "We don't open for another half hour."

I stared at him. "The hot dogs and hamburgers will be burned by then," I pointed out, in case he hadn't noticed that they were ready to eat now.

"These are for us. We don't open to the public until noon," he snapped back.

"My grandson is starving, couldn't I buy just one of these hot dogs," I begged, holding back the anger that was building in my normally even tempered disposition.

"No way lady, come back at noon and stand in line with everyone else."

That did it. Mild mannered MeMe had been pushed too far.

"At least you could be nice about it. I haven't met one nice person since I got here." This guy, and the others, who had now turned around, were going to get the brunt of my day-long frustrations, whether they liked it or not. Only a hot dog could have kept me quiet, and they didn't offer, so I let them have it. Of course I should have gone to the manager with my complaints, but I figured there'd probably be a line there, as well.

When I finished indicting the whole ski slope operations, and all the people who had been so rude, I grabbed Tommy's hand and dragged him off to find a candy machine.

By the time we got back to the slopes the ski instructor was bringing the other children in from their lesson.

"Did you have a good time?" I asked.

"Yeah," they all said. "But we're really hungry, MeMe."

Five hours after we arrived, $150 poorer, I packed five bedraggled, hungry urchins into the car and headed home, stopping for a very late lunch. (You didn't think I was going back to that ski slope outdoor grill, did you?)

Trying to save the day, and continuing my role as a generous grandmother, I said, "Order anything you want, this is your day."

"I'd like a soft crab sandwich," said Jay. I looked at the menu — soft crab sandwich — $6.95.

"So would I," said David. Now I knew that Jay liked crabs but I was sure that David didn't. I've hardly ever seen David eat anything but a plain cheese sandwich, with absolutely nothing on it.

"David, you don't like soft crabs. How about a cheese sandwich," I urged.

"No, I want a soft crab," he said, sounding confident about his decision. I knew in my heart that David only wanted a soft crab sandwich because Jay did. But I let him order it, against the better judgement that grandparents often ignore.

In case you don't know, soft crabs are fried with shells, claws and feelers all in place. I had a feeling David didn't know that. The expression on his face, when the waitress put the sandwich down in front of him, proved me right. He just stared at those two pieces of bread with spider-like claws and feelers sticking out the sides. No way he was going to take even a little bite.

"Would you like my hamburger?" I asked.

David looked at me with a sheepish look of repentance and nodded his head yes.

As we drove home in silence I found myself wondering whatever happened to uncrowded ski slopes, reasonably priced lift tickets, nice people, and peanut butter and jelly sandwiches.

Dining Room Table

Seasons bring change, some of which I would just as soon live without. There is no getting away from this certain annoying fact of life. I've tried without success and a lot of aggravation. I can't ignore it. It's here, not outside my window, but inside my house, in everyone's view, on the dining room table. You can tell what season it is by simply walking into my dining room, and looking at the table.

Just when the Christmas cards, wrapping paper, and chocolate candy with their bottoms pushed in are cleared away, and I think, "Oh good, let's have a dinner party," along comes my least favorite time of the year. Tax time means that folder after folder of half-kept records come out of the closet, and onto the table, providing misery as well as mess. The stacks of documents, and bits of torn paper with important information that no one can decipher, remain scattered nervously from one end of the table to the other for weeks, sometimes months.

Every year I say this is the year I'm going to keep precise, accurate records of what I spend and when. I'm going to know where I drive and what for. I'm going to have a ledger of which bills are for business and which ones are personal. Just once I'd like to avoid that belittling, patronizingly polite look on my husband's face that says, "If a woman doesn't take the time to balance her check book she should be denied a driver's license, and any job of responsibility that requires even the slightest bookkeeping."

It is this time of year that I try to find alternate routes to the kitchen. I've been known to go out the side door and in the back door, in the middle of a snow storm, just so I won't have to pass *that man* sitting at my dining room table trying to make sense of my yearly records.

The only solution is an accountant. Although most accountants are male, men are more patient and solicitous when they are being paid. And the best part in hiring an accountant, male or female, is that he or she wouldn't work at my dining room table.

Egg Hunt

Money can't buy happiness but it sure can help keep the children close to home. Using that philosophy, several years ago, I designed an Easter egg hunt for my grown children and their families and now I can always count on having my whole family spend Easter with me.

There are Easter egg hunts using colorful plastic eggs, and those with the real thing, colorful dyed hard-boiled eggs that usually end up squashed, revealing the unappetizing whites that have taken on the hue of the dye in which they were dipped, soaked or dropped.

My egg hunt includes both the plastic eggs, and the real eggs that my grandchildren have not so carefully colored.

It also features special eggs, eggs of incentive I call them. In many of the plastic eggs, which pull apart, I put coins. From fifty cent pieces to shiny new pennies. In some I slip a dollar bill. In at least one there is a five dollar bill.

Then there is the golden egg with a ten attached, so well hidden that I have to give one of my now famous (at least in the family) rhyming clues.

> This egg is hidden in a place so hard
> Like an old and rusty bucket of lard
> That's where to find the gold
> And the money to fold.

The top prize is called the Super Egg. It contains a gift certificate from a nearby clothing store. There is also a big yellow egg that I call the fool's gold. This egg is usually out in the open, but in a place hard to reach, like up in a tree. The egg hunters never know, until after they have risked life and limb getting it, whether the fool's gold contains real money or play money.

After all the eggs have been found there is a ham and turkey to go with the squashed eggs and high spirits.

Some may call such an egg hunt a bribe. I call it an investment in the most important institution I've come across yet — The Family.

State Fair

Some people love to go to the State Fair, each summer, for the midway and cotton candy, the amusement rides and Polish sausage sizzling on the greasy grill. (Now that's Americana!)

Some people go to the fair to see the largest squash, or peaches perfectly preserved. The sheep shearers get their fair share of attention. These are men and women who artistically remove a sheep's entire fleece as quickly, as easily as the rest of us take off a sweater.

The enticement for others is to watch horses and ponies being put through their paces under the amazingly strong and graceful control of children.

The tractor pull and taffy pull always attract large audiences, who like sticky situations.

What I find most appealing about the State Fair are the fresh, wholesome, corn-fed kids, and I don't mean goats. I'm talking about the young people who live and work down on the farms, coming to the fair once a year to share with the rest of us their way of life.

These are young men and women who have learned to care for their animals before ever worrying about themselves. As you watch these kids working in the barns, washing down their cows, cleaning stalls, you won't see designer clothes or trendy tennis shoes. You'll see very little, or no, make-up on the rosy cheeks of the girls sleeping in the straw. You'll see almost no nail polish.

What you will see are strong hands that have known lots of work. You will also see the clear eyes that result from "early to bed; early to rise." You'll see future farmers, and homemakers. You'll see the kind of hard working, God fearing, community service youth who built this country and made it strong; kids who give us all hope for the future, no matter where we live or what we do.

Off-Season

The wind blows out of the northeast, flags flutter against a smog free sky of surfboard blue. The almost clear green water rolls in on an unraked beach filled with pebbles, shells, and abandoned debris. The people on the beach no longer outnumber the sea gulls. It's off-season at the seashore.

There are people, but not the crowds of summer; the sound of paddleball being played can still be heard, but without the life guard's whistle bringing it to an abrupt end; a man runs with his dog along the water's edge. There's something wonderful about being at the ocean in the fall of the year.

The cool days are refreshing when you're outfitted in long pants and a sweat shirt.

The occasional warm days you devour with the passion of lovers about to be parted.

You linger on the beach, cuddled in the sand, soaking up the warmth of the autumn sun before it's blown away by the winter winds.

Off-season means no lines at your favorite restaurant and half price sales are advertised in almost every shop window. It's a world free of flies and jellyfish; and long forgotten are the raucous young people, some call June Bugs, over-celebrating their high school graduations.

The pressures are few. The demands to do something, to see something, go somewhere are almost non-existent in the adult world of off-season at the seashore. Watching the tide come in and go out can take all day. Every year I like to have two weeks at the beach. One during the summer with the children and all the grandchildren, and one with just my husband during off-season.

If I could have only one week — which would it be?

Oh, please, please don't make me choose.

Inconsiderate Drivers

Driving to and from the beach, and driving around Maryland as much as I do, it dawned on me that something terrible happens to many people when they get behind the wheel of a car, truck or mini-van, and I don't understand why. These are perfectly sane people who go to church or synagogue, who contribute to charities, who are kind to family and friends. But when they get out on the public roadways, they turn into self-centered, uncaring, motion-motivated maniacs.

A man who lives off of Route 50 on Kent Island, the main route to most Maryland, Delaware, and Virginia beaches, told me about helping a Baltimore motorist who was heading for Ocean City. The driver had a flat tire, and this local resident changed it. The motorist asked how he could reward the man. "Just slow down and give me a chance to get out of my driveway the next time you're traveling this way," he said.

Few drivers seem to think about the communities they drive through or the people who live there.

Finksburg, near my home, is located on the densely traveled, often deadly, Route 140. The opening of Interstate 795 which feeds into 140, has made it even worse. Drivers speeding through this area seem to forget that this is a hometown community for the people who live here. There is a post office and people want to go there. There are two banks, a fruit stand, a small shopping center, and some very nice people. But most motorists don't seem to care. They just want to get from point A to point B as fast as possible, and God forbid any local yokel gets in their way. Horns honk and fists are raised.

And, another thing, why can't other drivers respect someone trying to drive the speed limit? Driving the interstate between Baltimore and Washington D.C., safely, is a death defying act.

When I get on this road I'm usually driving 55 mph, the posted speed limit. When I get off I'm always up to 65 or 70, and my nerves are as revved up as my car's engine.

Driving 55 on I-95 would be like driving a kiddy car in the Indy 500. People pass you like you're standing still. Actually that would be fine if they'd just pass you, they don't, they run up behind you at 70 or 80, dart around you to the left and the right, they honk their horns like you're the one doing something wrong. How dare someone actually drive the speed limit. These are cars as well as trucks, big tractor trailers, bearing down on you from behind, swerving to avoid rear-ending you. Eighteen wheelers swinging around you and heading on down the road in a cloud of diesel smoke and burning rubber to terrorize some other poor idiot trying to obey the law. Driving 55 on I-95 is paramount to giving in to an early death. A person must drive faster to be safe. For thirty minutes, when I'm traveling to D.C. on I-95, I become a race car driver in a four-wheel drive Jeep Cherokee.

Why is there no patience on the highways? Where is the courtesy of caring for our fellow man, woman, child, and pet who might try to cross the road?

Where motorists enter Maryland from neighboring states there are signs posted that say *"Welcome to Maryland — Drive Gently."* Perhaps they should be repainted to read, *"Drive Like The Human Being You Were Before You Got Into That Vehicle."*

Out of the Mouths
of Grandchildren

I was cleaning out a drawer and 5-year-old Jay was watching me. Some of the things went right in the waste basket. The others I was putting aside to put neatly back in the drawer.

My passport was on the top of the pile to go back in the drawer. Jay picked it up. "What's this MeMe?" he asked, as he began to look through it.

"That's my passport," I answered knowing what the next questions would be.

"What's a passport?"

"Well," I began slowly, searching for an explanation that he would understand. "It proves that I'm an American citizen. Whenever I travel out of the country I have to take this with me so that the people there will know who I am and where I'm from. I also need the passport so that I can come home to America without any trouble. I don't have to carry the passport all the time, only when I go to a foreign country."

"Like Ocean City?" Jay asked seriously.

"Not exactly," I said, wondering where to go from there. All this time I've been thinking that it would be questions about sex that would stump me.

7 "Grand" Mother Nature

There's green in them thar hills.
It's not money. It's far more
important. It's life.

Earth Day

In April of 1990 the country celebrated the twentieth anniversary of Earth Day. For many people, Earth Day, twenty years ago, was the beginning of the environmental movement. It brought about public awareness and concern for the health of our planet. Large numbers of people started asking, "What can we do to protect our world, to preserve it, to use its wealth of resources without abusing them?"

Good questions; good movement.

For me, however, the environmental movement has not affected my basic feelings about the earth and our responsibility toward it. My deep seated love of our lush land and its bounty were taught to me a long time ago, as a child, by my mother and father. The lessons were more by example than by words. These two people taught me that our responsibility to this thing we call earth is to respect it, to give back, to make it a little bit better than when we arrived here.

I watched my father take an old run down farm, and turn it into one with tree-lined meadows, and tall alfalfa fields. On his days off from his regular job he worked the farm from sun up to sun down, clearing the land and then planting and mowing. He knew and loved every inch of this land, with the same unreserved commitment and pride that he loved his wife. The flaws and faults, the steep hills and stony earth became as endearing to him as the smooth green pastures and surrounding blue lake. Just as with the woman he loved, the beauty he admired was in all the qualities that made up the overall character.

I watched my mother dig her not so well manicured hands into soil made rich by compost and manure, planting flower bulb after flower bulb, which continue to bloom today.

My mother and father no longer live on this earth but the piece of this planet which was under their care, while they did, is richer and more beautiful because, for them, every day was earth day. And so it is for me.

Fish Pond

My father and mother did do most of the work to turn a run down farm into a property of which we can now be proud. Of course, those of us who still live here have fields and lawns to mow, fences to repair and replace, but for the most part, it is as they left it.

However, carrying on the tradition they established, we do keep adding little things that continue to improve our land. My daughters have put in new flower gardens, and I recently put in a fish pond, or water garden as they're now being called.

It was a lot of work, but worth it. I hand dug the 14' x 9' free form pond that is only 18 inches deep at the deepest part. Even so, it required the removal of tons of dirt.

I impulsively decided to do this project one weekend when my husband was involved with a business project and couldn't help. But, once I start something there's no stopping me or slowing me down. Besides, the more work, the more sense of reward if it turns out right. The fish pond turned out better than I dared hope.

After the almost back-breaking work of digging out the dirt, installing the liner and edging the pond with rocks, I began to savor the rewards of my labor. First, when I filled the pond with water it didn't leak. Then I added the plants, water lilies, iris, grasses, and mint. Then came the gold fish, six of them, one for each grandchild.

The end result is the most peaceful, pleasurable addition to our family farm that I have experienced in fifty years.

I find myself drawn to the pond the first thing in the morning, with a cup of coffee, to watch the fish become active, to see the water lilies open.

The pond was quickly adopted by a princely frog I named Jim, respectfully so, after the late Jim Henson whose first and perhaps most famous puppet creation was Kermit the frog. It's always fun to try and find Jim's latest hiding place. It's very difficult to find a greenish brown frog in a greenish brown pond.

I could simply sit and gaze at the flowers and the water, watch the fish, and look for the frog for hours. This is something I've never done before. With a regular flower garden there are always weeds to pull. With a swimming pool there's always something that needs doing to keep it clean. With my water garden there are no weeds to pull, no filters, no chemicals to add. The algae is part of the balance of its natural state. I feel a sense of ecological harmony staring into the pond. The aching muscles, from building it, have long gone. What's left are years, I hope, of long lovely lazy hours of serenity and contemplation, and no work.

Afterthought: When I finished recording this piece at the radio station, the engineer doing the taping said, "Susan, you need to get a life."

To which I said, "This is a life, the life I've been seeking for the past 50 years."

The Outer Banks

In June of 1990 I met a couple traveling down the southeast coast of the United States. It was the second time they had made this trip.

The first time was back in 1975. This husband and wife, and their two young children, had packed up the car with beach blankets, bathing suits, peanut butter sandwiches and headed down the coast to the outer banks of North Carolina. It was a vacation the couple never forgot. They remembered with unfading clarity the solitude and isolation of what seemed like endless sand dunes; the wild horses roaming free; the light houses and the ferry ride to the island of Ocrakoke.

That's where I met them, fifteen years later. The children were now grown, so the parents decided to make this trip again, without the kids.

As the ferry boat carried us across the sound, the woman, sitting on the trunk of the family car, leaned back against the rear window to soak up the sun.

"It's all grown up now, just like our children," she said, reflecting with sadness on the development that had occurred since they last visited the Carolina Coast.

"There're houses now where there used to be horses. Big houses!" She was referring to the multi-million dollar developments that have transformed the northern end of the outer banks into a sea of extraordinarily beautiful and expensive mansions. What was once pristine now boarders on the profane.

Yet there is still much rustic beauty to be seen on the Atlantic Coast and this woman told me that she hopes to make this trip again, in another five years. But she says that she doubts that their grown children will ever have any desire to repeat the trip that they made as kids.

She said, with melancholy, "Kids today don't know how to enjoy the simple pleasures of life. Peanut butter sandwiches aren't good enough anymore and sand dunes, sea gulls, abandoned light houses just don't appeal to a generation used to the instant gratification of electronic entertainment."

Well, I can only hope that someday young people will rediscover the pleasures of simple things, the joy of nature, before it's all paved over and only available as an electronic memory on video tape.

May Flowers

Florists tell us to "Say It With Flowers." They want us to let a gift of flowers convey our love, caring, and concern. I often do that, let flowers speak for me, but certain flowers also speak to me, because of the people I associate with them.

For example, daisies say, "It's the thought that counts." It was long before Jack and I were married, when we were working together as TV reporters, when our love was new. Once, while out covering a story, Jack stopped along the road to pick some wild daisies to give to me. It was a hot summer day and he left them in the car while he did the story. Hours later he walked into the newsroom and ceremoniously handed me what had become a bunch of wilted and forlorn looking daisies. They were drooping down over his fist as he said, "I hope you believe it's the thought that counts." I carried daisies when we were married.

Lilies say, "You're very special."

My mother loved lilies, and grew them well. She loved them all, but she often took a single lily and put it in an antique glass bottle to display in our home. She believed that sometimes you need to single out the individual flower so that it can be noticed for its own specialness, not just as one of a bunch. This former school teacher taught me that people, especially children, need to be treated the same way.

Black-eyed Susans say, "I love you."

My son used to pick Black-eyed Susans and give them to me. From the early years of youthful innocence, through early adolescence, until the year he died at age seventeen, he never outgrew the desire to pick Black-eyed Susans and bring them to his Mom. Black-eyed Susans now grow on his grave.

Flowers speak when words seem hard.

Out of the Mouths
of Grandchildren

Three-year-old Tom was looking at, and testing, the creams and lotions on my bathroom counter. This is something he loves to do. Several weeks earlier he had tried to pump some lotion from one of the bottles, nothing came out because it was almost empty. I explained that I needed to buy some more.

This time he tried the same bottle and lotion squirted out freely covering his hand.

"Oh, you got some more cream," he said, his eyes lighting up. I had almost forgotten the incident with the empty bottle, but Tommy hadn't.

"You're so smart," I said praising his memory.

His smile became a frown as he squinted up his eyes. "No I'm not," Tommy said angrily, taking offense to a word he didn't understand. I tried again, "I mean you have a lot of brains in that head of yours."

Tommy's look softened. "I know that," he said, "that's why I have to wash my hair when I take a bath."

8   Looking Inward

There's a time to live and a time to die.
A time to give, and a time to think
about yourself.

A Time to be Selfish

I met a woman on a plane recently who started me thinking about how and what parents give to grown children. I don't mean pitching in and helping when there is a real need. I mean giving money and luxury items that they could well do without until they could afford to buy them on their own. It seems that there are many women these days who, along with their husbands, have worked hard to create a good life for themselves and their families, but who still feel the need to go on providing, in a generous way, for their adult children. These are grown children who no longer live at home, some are married, some not, but all are out on their own.

It's an effort, I think, to make their lives happier and less stressful than ours was at their age. We also go on giving material things to try and show our love.

There's no question that this woman on the plane could well afford to go on giving, but she was questioning whether she should. She was a woman in her fifties, a lovely blonde, tanned and smartly dressed. She wore gold jewelry and a large diamond ring. She had inviting blue eyes and I found her to be as warm and open as her frequent laugh.

She and her husband were flying into Maryland to visit their married daughter and her family, which of course, meant their grandchildren. The woman had called her daughter just before she got on the plane to make sure she remembered to pick them up at the airport. Her eye got moist with emotion as she spoke. Tears of pain, not joy.

"They'll be here to meet us," she said, "but it's just one more thing that they have to do today. They have such a busy life and they do have their own life, and that's the way it should be," she went on, I think trying to convince herself more than me.

"It's just that I didn't hear any excitement in my daughter's voice. It didn't sound as if she were really looking forward to seeing us. It seemed a bother that she had to come to the airport." Her voice trailed off. She paused and then began again, as if thinking out loud. "We give our kids so much. Why do we do it?" she questioned. "Private school for the grandchildren, membership in a country club. Do they really need it? Does it even make them happy? Sometimes I think they even resent it. Like we still have control over their lives, and we expect them to pay us back — like coming to pick us up at the airport." The hurt again rose to the surface and filled her eyes.

Before ending the conversation, this woman told me that she thought it was time to be a little less generous to the kids, and a little more selfish. She explained that her husband had been thinking about early retirement and that they were seriously considering selling everything, and moving to Florida.

Another woman in her fifties shared similar feelings with me. She and her husband have always dreamed about going to Europe, not to live, just for a vacation. They have budgeted and saved for years for this trip. They thought that after the children were grown and educated it would be easy to do, but it seems each time they get close to having enough money, one of the married children needs something.

A car breaks down and a new one needs to be bought; they help out.

A nursery needs to be furnished; they furnish it. They just haven't learned how to say no. They want their children to be happy. They want to ease their struggle, and help get them on their feet.

"But now," says this woman, "the time has come to do this for us. Who knows how many more years my husband and I have left to enjoy each other, and life, in good health. We're going to learn to say no to our kids," she says almost defiantly, "and we're going to go to Europe."

I hope that both woman will do what they say and learn to give less, so that they might realize their dreams while they're young enough and healthy enough to enjoy them. But I also suspect that the giving and sharing of what they and their husbands have earned and accumulated over the years won't stop altogether.

There is something about mothering, and wanting your children to have not only as much, but more than you had, that's hard to control, even when your children are grown.

And when you've been blessed with success that brings with it material things, you quite naturally want the children to share in that success, no matter what their age.

My mother never stopped giving to me. Never did I go on vacation that she didn't quietly push a check into my hand and say, "Buy yourself something special," or "Have a nice dinner." If I had a good time, and had nice things to enjoy, it made her happy. I've found myself doing the same for my daughters.

My mother's mother didn't do that for her because she didn't have any extra to give. Though my grandfather was a doctor, he was a country doctor who often got paid with chickens and fresh vegetables.

Don't let me mislead you — my grandparents had a good life, and they provided college educations for my mother and her two brothers. One of her brothers also became a doctor. But they didn't have a lot of extra money for luxuries. They scrimped and saved and budgeted, and when their children were married and out on their own, they were on their own.

In fact in those days — the 1920s, '30s and '40s, the trend was for married children to give to their parents.

Today we don't give our children a chance to do that, but I do think we should at least let them experience the rewards of earning things for themselves.

Having said that I can think of all kinds of things and experiences I'd love to be able to give to my kids. I guess it's a good thing I can't afford to do it.

I've never come back from a wonderful vacation that I haven't wanted to go back with the whole family; or even send them on their own. It's enjoying something and wanting those you love to know the same pleasure. And it would give me great joy to share such an experience with my family; to see them enjoying themselves in such surroundings.

Each summer I do take the entire family to a rented beach house for a week, and though hectic at times, I love it. And I love being able to provide this vacation for the children and grandchildren.

I guess the answer, as with most issues, is in moderation. To know when the giving is really needed and appreciated, and satisfying for all involved. And to know when to say no, and when it's time to be a little selfish.

Being Alone

It seems to me that women don't much like being alone. We tend to go to the ladies room in groups, or at least in pairs. When women go out to dinner with friends, or as part of a party of mixed couples, one woman will always announce to the other women at the table, "I'm going to the powder room. Would you like to come along?" All the women get up and leave the table. To a spectator it looks as if the women heard a fire alarm that the men didn't hear. Now you know they all didn't feel "the urge" at just that same moment.

Perhaps it's because we were told as girls that there is safety in numbers. We didn't go to the movies alone. If we didn't have a date we went with a group of girls. However, with some of the dates I had I would have been much safer alone.

With women's liberation and equality, seeing a woman alone is no longer as rare as it once was. Nevertheless, there are still places and situations where we stick out as if we're rejected females and we feel just as uncomfortable. At least I do, and so do many of my friends.

Rarely do I go out at night alone, but there are times when it is necessary. Most often it's for speaking engagements, some of which are out of town. Whatever the reason, whenever I've gone into a nice restaurant alone I've always felt conspicuous. "Is there just one?" the waiter will say with a note of disdain. A woman alone in a bar is really suspect.

Going to a reception or cocktail party where you don't know anyone is another example of feeling very alone in a crowd.

On the other hand being all alone on a beach, without another person in sight, can be very calming and comforting. As someone, way before me said, "Being alone and being lonely have little relationship to one another."

I cherish my time alone. It's how I've gotten to know me; to learn what I like about myself, and what I don't. It's when I determine if change or acceptance is called for.

I also now seek solitude to write. I worked in a TV newsroom for twenty-two years and wrote daily broadcast reports. It took a great deal of concentration to shut out the noise of two-way radios, news wire machines, and high energy people pursuing breaking stories and trying to make broadcast deadlines. It wasn't really fun.

But to be alone with one's thoughts, a pad of paper and pen is very satisfying, and therapeutic I might add. I highly recommend it for everyone, no matter what avenue your writing takes. Essays, poems, prose, or fragmented thoughts. Writing serves as a cleansing process for the mind, and you never know what you might end up with that you may want to share with other people.

Women aren't the only ones who shy away from aloneness. My husband turns the TV on whenever he's home; morning, noon or night, mostly for companionship. He's usually doing other things, like shaving or eating breakfast or reading the newspaper, but the television is on. As soon as he leaves I turn it off to be alone with my thoughts. How can we think things out if we're always letting other people fill our head with sounds and words and their thoughts.

I've learned that there is a time for sharing, and a time to discover the inner strengths and creative juices, and the personal power that can surface from spending time alone.

9 Age of Acceptance

We can't go back, even if we
wanted to, so why fight it.
Let's plunge on into our second
half century as if we belonged there,
and make it what we want it to be.

Out of the Mouths
of Grandchildren

Age and what seems old often depends on our point of view. A three year old child, three feet off the ground, can be a little short sighted.

I can remember thinking as a child, that my one set of living grandparents were ancient. As a matter of fact my mother and father, who got a late start marrying and having children, seemed old to me. My father was 36 when I was born, my mother 34. My grandparents were in their mid-sixties, and they looked like the Norman Rockwell sterotypic grandparents, with gray hair and wire rim glasses, so I can understand how I thought of them as very old. But I certainly didn't think my grand-children viewed me that way — until one day we started talking about age. Seven-year-old Emily questioned, "How old are you MeMe?"

"How old do you think I am?" I asked. Three-year-old Tommy, who was listening started guessing.

"Five, seven, ten," he rattled off, throwing out ages and numbers familiar to him. I smiled and shook my head, no.

"Twenty-five," said Emily.

"No-o-o," I said as if that was a silly guess, but feeling flattered to be placed in an under-thirty age bracket even by a child.

"What's twenty-five plus twenty-five?" I asked this second grader.

She thought for a minute then a look of shock came across her face. "You're fifty?" she said incredulously.

"Yes," I admitted with some hesitation, hating to shatter my granddaughter's youthful image of me.

Then Tommy, who had been quietly listening to this exchange, blurted out, "MeMe, were there dinosaurs around when you were a little girl?"

Tina Turner Turns Fifty

Did you hear or read that Tina Turner recently celebrated her 50th birthday? That ball of energy in a mini skirt with the wild hair and seductive voice is half a century old.

I wonder if she's been notified by the American Association of Retired Persons that *she* is now eligible for membership and benefits in that organization.

And, I wonder if when she does get that letter with AARP boldly stamped on the envelope, if someone in her family, like my stepson did with mine, will put it up on the refrigerator with snide little comments attached like, "Getting up there aren't you Tina Baby," and "Maybe they have good deals on wheelchairs that rock as well as roll."

Now you know, by this time, that I'm proud to be a grandmother. And I'll tell anyone that I turned fifty in

August of 1990. But, like Tina Turner, I'm far from being a retired person, and I wasn't ready for that letter of membership in the AARP. I don't care how much money it will save me.

Well, maybe I do. But wouldn't Tina and I be more likely to join that organization if they sent the invitation in a plain brown unmarked wrapper so that some smart aleck teenager wouldn't be tempted to act as if he were living with Whistler's mother!

The AARP aside, I say hooray for Tina Turner for going public with this age milestone. Because if someone as hot as Tina Turner, still singing, stomping, and acting sexy, can be fifty maybe there's still some life left in old stepmom after all.

Meta Joy Turns Fifty

I went to a fiftieth birthday celebration recently, a surprise party for "a girl" I went to school with in high school. She was, in my eyes, the prettiest, most popular girl in school.

She had a baby doll face, big eyes, full lips, a turned up nose, and dimpled chin. Her skin was creamy smooth, and never did I see it blemished by nasty adolescent pimples like the ones all the rest of us tried to cover with Clearasil. And yes, even at age twelve she had a figure, that just got better every year. She also had a great personality. Girls as well as boys liked her. You might be envious, but you couldn't dislike her. Meeting her family made you like her even more.

She was Meta Joy Foell, daughter of Elsa and Eddie Foell who owned Foell's Meats in Baltimore's famous

Lexington Market. To top it off she had a handsome brother, Tom.

Meta Joy had it all. She was the kind of girl who had lipsticks in ten different colors, when I was trying to convince my parents to let me have one. *Her* parents understood!

Meta Joy was one of those girls who wanted to change her name; didn't we all, only *she* did. She called herself Kandi, and it stuck.

Now perhaps you think this commentary is going to end by my telling you that, at age fifty, justice has prevailed and that someone that pretty and poised and popular as a girl has lost it with age. Well, justice has prevailed, and someone that nice is still beautiful, proving that fifty can be fabulous.

It's now fun to think about all my childhood heros and heroines who are fifty: Snow White, Scarlett O'Hara, Tina Turner, and Meta Joy Foell — I'm in some good company.

Let's Talk

I wrote the preceding commentary about Meta Joy turning fifty after I received an invitation to her fiftieth birthday party. I recorded it at the radio station where I was working at the time and gave her a copy of the tape as a present.

On Monday morning following the party the commentary was aired, during my regular broadcast time, for the general public to hear. Several days later I got a note from Meta Joy. With her permission I share part of it with you.

Dear Susan & Jack:

Wow! I don't know where to begin . . . I was so *totally* surprised that such a party could be pulled off! I was so excited to see you two there. I've thought about you and your family so many times over the years. I read your book, Susan, and cried. I thought about contacting you/and didn't. You know what they say about the road to hell being paved with good intentions . . . my thoughts and prayers were with you/you just had no way of knowing that!

I can't begin to tell you how overwhelmed (really) I was with your birthday gift. To find out after all these years that the girl I turned green with envy over was thinking that I was all the things I *knew* she was . . . Does that make sense? What a riot! I keep listening to that tape saying to myself, "Me? Susan felt that way about me?" Wow, what a tribute on *any* birthday, but especially the fiftieth when we're beginning to feel a little insignificant. You *absolutely made* my birthday the *best* ever! Thank you so much. There's so much I'd like to say — to talk about/Suddenly I want to tell you everything I've been thinking since we last had a conversation — 35 years ago! Let's *try* to get together — you know "do" lunch — or dinner — or drinks — whatever works.

Love, Meta Joy (Kandi)

Isn't it funny; actually not funny but sad, that as girls Meta Joy and I admired and envied one another, but we never told each other then. If we gave a compliment to one another it was something we thought we should say, and was usually very superficial.

"Oh, that's a great pink poodle skirt."

Somehow, we must have felt that if we said what we really thought about each other, it would have revealed our insecurities and made the other person feel even more superior than we already thought she was.

As women of fifty, security has set in.

We have developed a sense of understanding, and humor, about who we are and what we are and what we're not.

And we have also learned that it feels good to compliment, and that there's room in this world for more than one attractive or appealing person. We're no longer competing for the attention of "Mr. Wonderful," the basketball star.

Today we can talk and laugh, and reveal the silliest things, and deepest doubts, with the same honesty. No longer do we feel threatened by someone who, we might think, has more to offer than we do.

We truly share in the joy of each other's successes and are pained by their losses.

High school rivals who never had a chance to really get to know each other at fifteen, have a real shot at becoming close friends at fifty.

And yes, Meta Joy, we *will* do lunch.

Growing Old Gracefully

"My idea of growing old gracefully is sneaking in through the back door of old age with a chocolate cream pie. I hope no one notices that I'm there, but if, or when they do, I'll have something to sweeten the moment for us all."

I want to set the record straight. Though I'm enjoying this period in my life, immensely, and I suspect it will be the best decade I live through, I don't dread becoming sixty or feel that my life will be over when I hit seventy. However, I'm also not in a hurry to get there. I'm not ready to be called a senior citizen, or even a golden girl. Actually, I hate labels of any kind, on people or clothes. I wish fashion designers would at least put their labels back inside their clothes.

In any case, I plan on dragging whatever youthfulness I can maintain right on into the next decade, and the next, for as long as I can. I'm still a blonde, by choice. I try to maintain a respectable figure, and I use lots of skin cream in hopes of avoiding additional wrinkles for as long as possible. *And* I now use sun block when at the beach. My chest would look twenty years younger if I had started doing that when I was twenty.

I don't intend to wear my age like a badge in hopes of getting in movies and museums for a discount. I have to admit that it's nice when someone thinks that I'm younger than I am.

The summer I turned 51 I took my six grandchildren to an amusement park at our favorite ocean resort. I was dressed in summer casuals; pink cotton pants and a loose, brightly colored cotton shirt. I had my hair pulled back in a pony tail with a bright pink tie. I was tan, and wore little make-up.

With that look, and six kids clinging to me, I "fooled the guesser" and won a teddy bear for one of the children.

This was one of those carnival hucksters who, for a dollar, tries to guess your age within three years. This guesser announced over the microphone, to a large ring of spectators, that though he hated to embarrass me publicly it was his job to tell the world that I was thirty-seven. You can bet *I* was ready to tell the world, beginning with my 58-year-old husband.

One of the great things about being fifty-something in the 1990s is that we can have it all.

We've all heard people say if I could go back to being twenty, knowing what I now know, I'd be a millionaire or great lover, or whatever else one dreams of becoming during the age of longing. Well, as a healthy, fairly well-kept fifty-year-old with the experience and knowledge that does only come with age, I feel like I'm in an even better position. Because I now realize that being a millionaire or great lover isn't the route to happiness. Nice but not necessary. Now, I'm not ready to discard everyone's dream of striking it rich someday, and I'm still working on being a great lover, but my life certainly doesn't hinge on either goal. Besides, it's true that getting there is half the fun.

I feel like I'm now able to enjoy all the things that this age has brought. The physical and emotional well-being, the intellectual curiosity; the deep love and sensitivity that has only come to me with age.

It is all these things that I hope to be able to continue as middle age becomes old age. As long as I have my health I'm not afraid of growing old, and I have every confidence that I can do it gracefully, with the help of a chocolate cream pie or two.

10 Health Watch

When you feel well, physically and
mentally, you can handle most
anything. When you don't —
lean on those who love you.

Come What May

In September of 1990 Jack and I went back to our favorite place in Somerset, Bermuda. It was a trip we really couldn't afford to take and if we'd been fiscally responsible we wouldn't have done it. I had just learned that the radio station carrying my commentaries was planning to drop them from the format. It is a mostly music station owned by a conglomerate in New York, and the out-of-town consultants advised the local management that they didn't need "Susan's People and Perspective" to attract listeners, in fact, it might even be a turn off for people wanting to listen to music and only music, and so I was fired. I'd never been fired before. It hurt and it stopped my one steady source of income, as modest as it was.

Jack was already working part time, free lancing, so neither of us had a regular income. The country was heading into a recession. It was not exactly sound judgement to dip into our savings to go to Bermuda. But we did, and looking back I'm extremely glad our instincts told us to "go for it."

The romance and the magic of that island once again enveloped us and freed us from the problems we were facing in the day-to-day existence of the real world. Our appreciation of each other and life dawned anew with each sunrise, and grew warm with passion each night. One night, before bed, sitting out under the stars, we talked quietly, holding hands, absorbed in the beauty around us and in the comfort of our companionship.

"Do you ever think about dying?" Jack asked softly, with more reflection than fear.

"Not very often," I answered. "It seems to be a waste of time. We're going to die someday, but why spoil what we have now by worrying about something that might happen years from now. We can't change what's eventually going to happen anyway. So why think about it?"

"We've had a good life together," Jack said, voicing his thoughts more than responding to my words. "I'd just like to have a lot more time with you," he continued, "for our life together." His words touched me deeply and my eyes filled with tears.

"I know what you're saying. I don't want what we have to end either, and I'm not ready to leave the kids on their own." My voice cracked as a smile tried to soften the seriousness of my words.

"There really isn't anything we can do about it except enjoy each day that we have," I went on.

Jack's head, that had been resting against the back of the chair as he stared out at the stars, turned toward me. Our eyes met through the darkness. His hand tightened around mine.

"I love you," he said, "come what may."

Almost exactly two months after that trip to Bermuda I was forced to think about dying, much sooner than I planned.

Life's like that, isn't it? Just when you think you've figured it out and can handle whatever comes along, a curve ball comes across home plate, and the game is no longer a sure thing. The curve ball I didn't see coming, sailed across my home plate on a cool windy November day, the Saturday before Thanksgiving.

Jack and I had been asked to anchor the telecast of the annual Baltimore Thanksgiving Day Parade. We were looking forward to working together again, on television. It is what both of us have found to be the most rewarding aspect of our careers. Whether it was sharing a news anchor desk, or co-hosting a telethon, or a talk show, there was a chemistry that emerged when we were together on TV that provided us with a personal high, as well as professional pride. Knowing one another as well as we do, and respecting each other's on-camera talents allows us to use that insight and instinct to occasionally step over the professional line usually drawn between two TV performers. As a result we can deviate from the script, kid one another, and go for the one liners. We have fun and apparently so do the viewers.

Such was not the case with this broadcast.

All live telecasts, especially ones on location, are stressful. This broadcast was more so than usual.

The anchor desk had been set up on a scaffolding 15 feet off the ground over-looking the main parade route in the inner harbor section of the city. There was a strong wind to contend with, blowing in off the water and funneling up Pratt Street to our location. TV people "going live on location" hate wind. It usually means their carefully coiffed hair will be wildly and often comically re-arranged before and during the broadcast. This isn't a small thing in TV news, for it seems that general managers of local TV stations will tolerate a reporter or anchor going on the air without having their facts straight, but not without having their hair or makeup in place.

However, mussed hair was not what concerned us with this broadcast. We were holding on with our fingernails, trying to keep the scripts and index cards, which contained all the information about each float and parade unit, from blowing away, and also trying to keep them from getting out of order. (It's a little disconcerting to be at home watching one float glide across the TV screen and hear some confused broadcaster read the description of what is obviously another one.) We were using our hands, arms, and coffee mugs to try to hold all those cards and papers in place. Adding to the problems, the anchor desk was facing the parade route with the primary camera in back of us. So every time we turned around to go on camera we had to secure the scripts and cards or grab them up in our gloved hands and take them with us, or sure enough they'd be gone when we turned back, and then we'd have little or nothing to say for the rest of the hour. There was no teleprompter with this telecast. We either ad libbed or read from those cards. I don't know if you've ever tried to talk about a parade for an hour without knowing anything about it, but I was fighting for my life to hold on to those cards.

And if that wasn't enough stress, the communications hookup was not working as it should.

We were wearing large earmuff-type earphones that should have done more than keep our ears warm.

They didn't.

We couldn't hear what the reporter in the street was saying. The only way we knew her report was over was by reading her lips on the monitor in front of us, when she said, "Now back to you, Susan and Jack."

We couldn't even hear each other. We were sitting side by side and couldn't hear what the other was saying. Instead of our words being transmitted through the system and back into our ears, the earmuffs, which weren't working electronically, were actually keeping us from hearing the words being spoken a foot away.

All we heard was the director, who would tell us when to face the camera, when to cue to a commercial break, and when we were coming back on the air. It was a nightmare, all the while we smiled and tried to converse as if everything was going as planned, and that we were having a wonderful time.

Fifty minutes into the hour telecast I started to feel the results of the stress aching in the middle of my back. And then, as if someone had hit me on top of the head with a sledge hammer, a headache as I've never experienced before erupted in the top of my head. It wasn't a headache that gradually descended upon me; not one that I felt coming on. This one exploded.

As I continued to comment and describe the parade passing before my eyes, I became aware of a feeling of nausea and weakness that I now believe was caused by intense pain, and the fact that I was pushing myself to continue with my on-air duties in spite of it. The smile was still on my face.

No one was aware of the agony I was experiencing. Not the director, or the camera operators, not even Jack sitting beside me. Mercifully, the show was coming to a close.

"I'm Susan White-Bowden," "And, I'm Jack Bowden. Thank you for joining us for Baltimore's annual Thanksgiving parade — brought to you by —." As Jack continued to talk I kept smiling. He would have to handle the close alone. He would get the message. If I just looked straight ahead into the camera and smiled he would sense that I wasn't going to say anything more. He did and I didn't.

"You're clear, we're off the air, good job, thank you very much." The director's voice penetrated the pain pounding and pulsating in my head. I pulled off the earphones and dropped my head to the anchor desk. Jack leaned forward. "What's wrong?" he asked with alarm.

"I don't know. I've got the worst headache I've ever had. Something awful is happening."

"Can you get down off this scaffolding?" he asked.

"I'll have to," I said, getting up and easing down the makeshift ladder. Jack said that he would go get the car. I knew I couldn't walk even a couple of blocks. I had to sit down, I wanted to lie down. I sat on the curb of the sidewalk, my feet in the gutter, my hands holding my throbbing head.

A panhandler staggered up the sidewalk toward me. He stopped at my side.

"Can you spare a couple of quarters for some food?" I looked up at him without speaking. "Hey, you're that lady on TV ain't you?" I nodded slightly. "You sick or something?" I nodded again.

"Never mind about the money," he said kindly and walked off. I smiled at his concern.

When I got home I took numerous over-the-counter pain killers and went to bed. I slept a while and when I woke the pain had subsided a little.

The next day, Sunday, though I didn't want to shake my head real hard, I felt pretty much back to normal. On Monday morning someone called to book a speaking engagement. I answered the phone downstairs and ran up the stairs to my office to check my calendar. After I ran back down the stairs to replace the receiver on the bedroom phone the pounding at the top of my head returned with the same suddenness and vengeance as it had done during the parade.

"Oh my God," I thought, "what is going on?"

I lay down and in about an hour the pounding stopped and the pain was gone.

I didn't tell Jack about this episode. I didn't want to worry him.

Tuesday I was fine.

Wednesday, before Thanksgiving, I got up to go to a Thanksgiving program at one of my grandchildren's school. The pulsating ache had returned.

This was clearly not just another headache. I, who like to downplay every potential health problem, believing that my body's very strong and can usually cure itself, had to acknowledge that something was very wrong inside my brain. Even so, I first went to the school program, then shopped for Thanksgiving dinner before I called the doctor.

"Let me describe what's been going on," I began, "and see what you think I should do."

When I finished, my doctor, Donald Wood, who is not an alarmist, sent me immediately for a CAT scan of my head. What he thought the scan might show was a brain tumor, or aneurysm that might have burst. But the brain scan looked normal. However, the headache persisted, and so did Dr. Wood. "Come into my office at 5:30 this evening, and we'll decide what to do," he said.

Jack had been working in Washington that day, and when he got home I told him what was going on, and concluded by saying, "Why don't I just go to bed, by tomorrow morning, I'll feel better. I'll fix Thanksgiving dinner and then Friday, I'll go to the doctor. I really feel too bad to drive into town anyway," I reasoned. All I wanted to do was lie down.

Jack rarely becomes impatient with my stubbornness but when it comes to my health he tends to take charge. He said that if necessary he and his son would tie me up and carry me to the car, but it was what else he said, only half in jest that moved me. "Let me tell you something," he began. "If you die tomorrow your grandchildren will always, and I mean always, remember that MeMe died on Thanksgiving Day. It will ruin that holiday for them for the rest of their lives.

I got up, got in the car, and Jack drove me to the doctor. Guilt can be a worthwhile tool.

First Doctor Wood discussed with us what might be causing my headaches. He thought perhaps the problem might be an aneurysm about to burst. An aneurysm is a bubble that has formed on the weakened wall of an artery. High blood pressure, vigorous activity or stress can cause such a bubble to break resulting in hemorrhaging, stroke, and about a fifty-fifty chance of death, or crippling brain damage. Dr. Wood decided, with our approval, that an angiogram should be done, immediately. Accomplishing this on Thanksgiving eve wasn't going to be the easiest task, but with Dr. Wood's aggressive take-charge attitude it happened.

The neurosurgeon at the hospital wasn't sure he wanted to do this potentially dangerous test without first getting the results of other simpler tests that might substantiate the need for such an invasive procedure. The angiogram requires that dye be fed into the arteries of the brain so that their shape, size, and condition show up as clear as a road map when X-rays are taken of the brain. This is done by inserting a tube through the groin that is then fed up inside the body and connected to each artery leading to the brain. The tube is moved from one artery to the other until all four of the arteries leading from the neck into the brain have been filled with dye and pictures taken. It takes about an hour-and-a-half to two hours to do. The danger lies in the fact that if a blood clot is formed, or one is loosened, and an artery becomes blocked, it could cause a stroke or death. Consequently, the decision to do such a test isn't made lightly, but Dr. Wood was insisting. He and the neurosurgeon were out in the hall debating the pros and cons of doing the test. "I know my patient," Dr. Wood was saying. "This isn't a hypochondriac. She doesn't complain. I never see her unless there is really something wrong. She's pinpointed the problem, and if she agrees to the test I want it done, tonight, before something happens that we can't repair."

Discovering an aneurysm before it ruptures gives doctors a chance to perform surgery to remove the bubble and repair the artery, providing the patient a much better chance of survival. Lying on the stretcher, in the emergency room of the Greater Baltimore Medical Center, I could hear the voices of the doctors discussing my fate.

Jack, standing by my side, leaned close to stroke my head with his hand. His fears were embedded in every line of his face. The tears he was trying so hard to control rimmed his eyes with redness and warned of the depth of pain that would follow should anything go wrong. In sympathy tears filled my eyes, not for myself, but for my husband. I wasn't afraid of dying; I never have been, but I know the pain of losing someone you deeply love, and I ached at the thought of Jack having to experience the agony of such a loss.

"What do you think?" he asked with uncertainty. "Do *you* think you should have this test?"

"What if I don't?" I said. "I don't want to walk around with a terrible headache, waiting for something worse to happen. I'd rather know if anything is really wrong, so they can do something about it, now."

He slowly nodded his head in agreement. "I don't want to lose you," he said softly, as if I could keep it from happening.

"I'm going to be fine," I said reassuringly. "If they can get rid of this headache, I'm going to be fine."

The neurosurgeon walked back into the room.

"If you're in agreement, we're going to proceed with the angiogram," he said.

"We're in agreement," I said looking at Jack and then turning to the surgeon for details.

It was about 11 p.m. when I was wheeled out of the emergency room, and into the radiology/X-ray department.

A nurse named Alverta came to get me. She was a handsome black woman with a deep honey-toned voice and a reassuring sense of humor. As she guided the stretcher out of the doorway and into the hall, Jack leaned over to give me one last kiss, and a few more words of reassurance. "Yeah, they always kiss the patient and they never kiss me," said Alverta pretending to be hurt. "Always the bridesmaid and never the bride," I quipped.

Jack straightened up quickly, and moved a few steps around the stretcher to where Alverta stood waiting. He put his arms around her and planted a big kiss on her cheek.

"Yeowee!" Alverta let out a squeal of delight that should have awakened half the hospital.

"I can't wait to tell my daughter," she yelled out as she happily pushed me down the hall. "Jack Bowden from television kissed me, right here," she sang out as she pointed to her cheek.

Two hours later, in the hospital room where I'd stay for the next four days, the neurosurgeon, looking very serious, was telling us what the angiogram revealed.

"The good news first," he said without a smile. "We didn't find an aneurysm. What we did find," he continued, "was a narrowing of some of the arteries in your brain."

As I understood it, the X-ray showed a sausaging effect, where the artery would start out normal and then narrow and then widen again. I was told that a clump of these narrowed vessels was located on the right side of the brain toward the top of my head, where the pain had been so intense.

When my blood pressure went up due to stress, the parade broadcast, exertion, running up the stairs, or strain, the increased blood backed up at the narrowed channels, and the result was the pounding and pulsating and severe headaches. In the heart when an artery becomes blocked and blood can't get through a heart attack occurs. When this happens in the brain a stroke occurs.

The doctor continued in a very straightforward manner, so that I would clearly understand the seriousness of the situation. "You came very close to having a stroke, but you didn't, and thanks to Dr. Wood for insisting that the angiogram be done, we now know what is causing the headaches and hopefully we can do something about it.

I learned that the condition is called vasculitis, and that it is a type of arthritis of the brain. There are many reasons such a condition develops, from hepatitis to an unknown, unexplained virus. After dozens and dozens of blood tests ruled out every known cause of vasculitis, the doctors went with the virus theory, admitting "we don't know why it happened." What they hoped would be the cure, no matter what the cause, was "corticosteroid," a miracle drug now used for many ailments that couldn't be treated before. The brand name most people know it by is Prednisone.

The down side of the drug are the side effects; weight gain, softening of bones, increased susceptibility to infection, mood changes, and many others. I was told, over and over again, that my life style would have to change, that I'd have to be careful and curtail some of my normal activities while on this drug for the next three months. "Don't lift heavy objects. Stay away from crowds and sick grandchildren. Don't eat fat and salt and high calorie foods."

When I left the hospital the Sunday following Thanksgiving, instead of being thankful that I was alive, and that I hadn't had a stroke, I was feeling like an invalid, and not taking it well. I've always been strong and self-reliant. I've never had to ask anyone to help me do anything. I didn't like the idea of being physically dependent on anyone for anything. On the way home I stared out of the car window noticing the homes with neatly raked yards. I knew the lawn around our house was covered with a thick carpet of maple leaves. I'd have to rely on Jack and Christopher to rake them up.

"Remember," Jack was saying, "the doctors said that you have to act as if you're a hospital patient, at home. You can't go home and just start doing all the things you did before. You really have to rest and take it easy, and let the medicine do its job." I didn't want to hear all this. I'd heard enough. I really didn't need a lecture.

I nodded my head, to let Jack know that I'd heard what he'd said, as I continued to look away from him and out of the car window. Tears now blurred my vision. I felt like a fool, a stupid, selfish ingrate. How could I feel sorry for myself when my life had been saved, and I would get well. I wouldn't always have to live with restrictions, as many people do, and do graciously. My reasoning wasn't working on me.

"I'm not going to live like an invalid," I choked out. "I'm not going to sit around and wait for you or someone else to do something that needs doing. You know how you are, you do things in your own good time, sometimes days after you decide something needs doing. I do things right away. I don't like to wait. It'll drive me crazy waiting for you to do something I could easily do myself. (All of a sudden what I'd written about "helping husbands" didn't seem so funny. I was losing my sense of humor along with my health and independence.)

"Look," said Jack, patiently but firmly, "you're alive, and I want you to stay that way. It's only for a few months and then you'll be back to normal. I'll change, you take it easy, and I won't put things off. I promise, you'll see."

"Yeah," I thought sarcastically, "I can really see that happening." Self-pity is an ugly emotion. Sitting beside me was a man who adored me and would do anything within his power to keep me alive. Waiting at home were two devoted daughters and sons-in-law and six grandchildren who would rally around me to make my recuperation as easy as possible. And there I was feeling sorry for myself. Maybe it was the medication. The doctors said it would affect my moods.

But I think more likely I was fighting something much more threatening than a few alterations to my day-to-day existence. I think I was refusing to face my own mortality. I said earlier that I wasn't afraid to die, and that I never have been. It's easy to say that when you don't believe it's going to happen. In my heart I didn't believe a medical test, even one as invasive as an angiogram, was going to kill me. But that test found something wrong, and if the medication didn't perform a miracle and return the arteries to normal, the vasculitis could get worse, the arteries could close up completely, and I could die. I didn't want to think about the possibility of that happening at the young age of 50, at the period in my life that I anticipated being the best. I think somehow I felt that if I gave in, and accepted the restrictions being placed on me by my doctors, and by my husband, that I was giving in to the approaching end. I wanted no part of that change. In my mind, if I went on and did everything I'd always done, and willed myself well, it would be so.

I've come to understand that sometimes we must alter our lifestyle in order to increase our life expectancy.

When I got home, though I hadn't stopped fighting my restrictions, I eased up a bit and started appreciating the day and those wonderful people I call family.

Jack and my children and grandchildren all congregated that afternoon to rake the leaves, so I wouldn't be tempted to do it. I think they did it to show me that there was lots of help available to do all those things I felt I needed to do.

The sun, strong for November, reflected off the golden leaves, those on the ground and those sent whirling through the air by fast moving rakes. There was a mellow glow of gold on the white barn and panel fences. The grandchildren squealed with delight and defiance as they jumped in the piles of leaves and pretended to hide from their impatient parents who were trying to get a job done.

I wanted to grab a rake, if not to help, just to join in the fun.

But I didn't, I watched and told myself there would be another fall.

11 Looking for Moonbeams

The darker it is,
the harder to find light.

Winter of Discontent

I sit and stare at the blank page. The words I need won't come. I'm left with a void, an emptiness of thought and creative reward. I'm sure it's the medicine, the "prednisone" that makes it hard to concentrate. Or is depression setting in.

It is January; outside a cold, dismal, uncomfortable rain is falling. Why couldn't it be snow? The grandchildren would be off from school. I'd hear their laughter and go to look; I'd feel better.

Snow softens the world, and the world needed softening. We were heading into a war, America was already into a recession. I hadn't worked since broadcasting the Thanksgiving Day Parade. Each day I looked in the mirror at the puffy cheeks and weight gain caused by the prednisone, and I'd think "it's a good thing no one has called."

Jack had had only one free lance narration job since December, and our video production business was at a standstill.

Christmas had been low budget. The fun part was that by trying to compensate it became more of an old fashion celebration. I baked cookies, we cut down our own tree; a skinny little pine Jack scouted in the woods at the edge of our property. The one extravagance I allowed myself, and the family, was Christmas eve dinner. It was wonderful.

I had the usual standing rib roast, which came out of the oven just right. Well done on the outside for both my sons-in-law, pink half way in for Jack, Christopher, and grandchildren, and really rare in the middle for my daughters and me.

It was one of those occasions where everything went right. The whole family was there, a feat in itself. And everyone was in a wonderful mood. No one had been arguing ahead of time, no one was exhausted, or sick or feeling undue pressure. The memory of that evening is among the best I have as a grownup; the food and wine, the Christmas lights, the poinsettia and red carnations, the laughter of the kids, the contented looks on the faces of the adult children who lingered, as if reluctant to leave. What mother of grown up kids doesn't savor that occasion when it occurs. All too often our children need or want to be somewhere else. There's so little time to talk, to share, to once again see Christmas light up their eyes, as it did when they were young.

Jack's son Christopher, now twenty, would be leaving for California after the holidays. Like so many kids he thinks perhaps the pot of gold at the end of his rainbow lies on the west coast. He'll either find it, or find that it's not there after all. But, as with all children who dream of another way of life, away from home, he must do the searching and make the discoveries, whatever they might be, on his own. And we, his parents, are left at home to endure the loneliness as he searches. No longer will we be nearby to share in the spontaneous joy of his successes, or to ease the pain of his disappointments.

His first test would be in trying to find a job. We hope there are more jobs in California than in Maryland. It seemed that more people were losing jobs than finding them.

I pick up the paper and start to read and article on the opinion page about being out of work, the emotional ordeal of applying for unemployment money. I look at the name of the writer. It's someone I know. Her father was an extremely well-known and popular radio personality who died in the spring of 1990. He had helped me get started in broadcasting. At the funeral this woman and I had talked and hugged and shared our own particular feelings of grief and sense of loss over her dad's death.

She had a good job then. How can it now be that she is so desperate to have to go through the humiliation of applying for public assistance? Why do I feel shame for her? I realize that if I weren't one of the lucky few to own a house without a mortgage and some savings to dip into I'd be sitting in that unemployment office with her. I call her on the phone. She sounds "up." "I've heard from so-o-o many people who read that article. It's been wonderful, and work's starting to come in. I got some part-time work last week, I had another article published, and I have a call-back interview with a publishing company in Pennsylvania for a job as an editor. I can't believe it. It's all happening at once." She was exuberant. "Now, if the person doing the hiring at that firm is out of diapers I might have a shot." She's even able to joke about the age factor, I thought. The article in the newspaper had said she had been replaced in her old job by a much younger person. "When I wrote that article I was at my lowest point, and now all this," she is continuing with the momentum of the relief she feels. "Mom said, when I was so down, that there was no where to go but up, and now I'm on the way up."

The pain and desperation that I read in the words of her article are gone from her voice.

I tell her how glad I am that things have changed so quickly, wish her continued good luck, and say goodbye.

I don't share my own melancholy. I don't have the energy, I don't want to bring her back down. Besides, she would find my situation impossible to believe. I know I do. I send out a resume for a speaking engagement, for which I won't be paid. It reads — award winning television reporter and radio personality — published author of two books — nationally known, critically acclaimed speaker on youth suicide prevention and surviving loss — chairman of a Government Commission — President of a production company. There must be some dollars in there somewhere, but there aren't, not in the winter of 1991. (I feel as if I'm sinking in a sea of achievement.)

I had been counting on a job with another television station in Baltimore, a Fox affiliate station that was scheduled to begin an hour newscast at 10 p.m., similar to what other Fox affiliates were already doing. In several conversations with the station's general manager, during the fall of 1990, I had been told that "they would be extremely pleased to have someone with my experience and popularity as part of that news cast." I had been lulled into a sense of security. I was telling myself, "get over the vasculitis, get through the winter, then in the wonderful warmth of spring, when new life begins, you'll be well and you'll go back to work."

Those secure feelings for the future were replaced with anxious uncertainly when I received a letter from the newly hired news director, from out of town. Aren't they all?

"I've decided to move in a different direction," he wrote. (News directors are always moving in a different direction. If it doesn't include you it's a different direction.) "I feel this station needs an entirely new look," he went on. And though he didn't come right out and say it, that meant without me. I guess he figured with all that experience as a reporter I could deduce that "a new look" doesn't mean someone who's been on the air for twenty years.

The good news in the winter of 1991, came when Jack was hired to work part-time for WJLA-TV, the ABC affiliate in Washington, D.C. He would be covering the Maryland Legislature and on his first day on the job, he was covering the Governor's inaugural address and swearing in.

It was 6 p.m.

I turned on the television to Channel 7.

Jack was reporting live.

He looked good. He sounded great. I was taping the report so he could assess himself when he got home. I left the TV on for the national news. A network reporter started talking about bomb blasts and tracer fire in Baghdad. Peter Jennings came back on the screen. He looked grim, but excited, like all news anchors do when they're about to tell us some history-making news for the first time.

"It appears that war has begun in the Gulf."

Watching a War on TV

"I don't know if the world should sit and wait, or what." Those words were spoken by a 14-year-old friend of our family. Ellen Barth is an active, involved teenager, who gets good grades in school, is an accomplished musician, an actress who has performed in local dinner-theatre, as well as opera at The Kennedy Center For Performing Arts in Washington, D.C. She is a very motivated young woman.

She is also a teenager who enjoys her family, and all the new adventures and challenges that each day of life brings to her world.

As the war in the Gulf unfolded and invaded the security of that loving, protected world, confusion set in for Ellen, as it did for us all.

"One night," she said, "I had so much homework to do, but I just sat there for three hours and watched the war on television." It's hard to go on with everyday things when our country is at war.

I think what Ellen needs to know is that as with any unsettling, perhaps even life-threatening adversity, we must go on with our day-to-day activities. It helps us maintain our sanity, and the normal world to which the combatants will return.

The week-end before the Gulf war broke out Barbara Bush was sledding with her grandchildren at Camp David. Unfortunately, the first lady broke her leg during the course of that afternoon. Nevertheless, she was helping her grandchild enjoy an afternoon of fun on a snowy hillside in the Maryland mountains, while she must have known war was about to erupt in the Middle East.

Life *does* go on, and without lying to our children about the seriousness of war, or some life-threatening illness a relative might be facing, they need to learn that while dealing with life and death matters, there can be, and should be, the diversion of enjoyment. It's very important that we continue our day-to-day activities, and not brood about what might happen. I also think that makes us better able to handle a crisis if, or when, it should occur.

American children of the '90s have never experienced the unsettling effects of war before. They know there have been wars that involved this country, from history books, and movies, but obviously that can't prepare them for living with a war day-to-day, not knowing what the outcome will be.

My granddaughter Emily, in trying to reassure herself, asked, "America has always won every war it's been in, hasn't it MeMe?"

"Not exactly," I had to say. "No one won the Vietnam War." I also had to add my feelings that, "There are no real winners in any war; only survivors who have to try and patch up the world and it's wounded, and put things back together." My words made me think of Humpty Dumpty and I thought, but didn't say, "One of these days all the king's men and all the king's horses aren't going to be able to put it back together again."

For some children, and adults, watching a war on television in the '90s is like watching the glitziest video game ever imagined. Accompanied by dramatic music, planes, bombs, and graphics race across the screen with a single touch of the TV remote control. And then, when we've had enough, we push the button again and turn off the war. Unfortunately, it's not so simple for the young men and women fighting and dying in that war.

In the tough competition for ratings, thus viewers, television newscasts, even before the war, had become well planned, well produced, slick presentations that wouldn't bore us or challenge our attention spans. Using all that technology, the news operations turned the war in the Gulf, also High Tech, into a fast paced dramatic entertainment series, complete with titles and a cast of celebrity reporters and generals.

Television is also the most intimate medium we have ever known; used properly it can convey images and feelings, emotions and messages that stay with us even after we turn off the set.

The courage and dedication of the young men and women in the face of possible death or crippling injury. The pain and worry with which their families must live every day. Also, what might be termed, "the collateral damage" of war, to borrow a euphemism used by the military to describe civilian casualties.

One Sunday morning Jack and I were watching a report about Arab-American families in this country and the mistreatment of these people that had begun as a result of the War in the Gulf. One family was being interviewed, explaining the pain they were feeling. They were American citizens, but they had family in Iraq, with family members in *both* armies. The woman was explaining that her nephew would soon be sent to the Gulf to fight. "For the United States?" the interviewer asked. "Oh yes," she said, "he's in the American army.

"So," said the interviewer, "it's conceivable that you could have family members on both sides of this war, fighting each other?" The woman nodded sadly.

The interviewer turned to the two young sons and asked if they were being treated badly at school, by the other kids, because of their Arabian heritage. The older boy, about 12 or 13, said he had been called names and some friends had stopped hanging around with him.

The interviewer then directed his question to the younger boy, about 8 or 10. The boy looked shy, embarrassed, reluctant to speak. As the camera tightened his handsome face filled the screen, we could see his dark brown eyes dart to the side, most likely searching for guidance form his parents who were sitting next to him, off camera. His gaze returned to the interviewer and he nodded that he too had been called names and shunned by some of the kids at school. The hurt showed in those innocent eyes as he blinked away the tears. Hesitantly and softly he spoke. "They say things like, 'we're going to really beat you today, you'll be sorry when we're finished with you'."

A lump formed in my throat as tears filled my eyes. I felt pain and anger. I wanted to take that child in my arms and say "Not all Americans hate you because your grandparents are Arabs."

I turned to Jack. "Why do we do that, why do we lump all people together? Why do all Arabs become Saddam Hussein; why did we make all Germans into Hitler; all Japanese, even those living in America, into the enemy? It's the shame of war."

"War brutalizes people," Jack began. "Look what the Germans did to the Jews, and what the Japanese did to other Asian countries, to whom they felt superior, and how horribly they treated the American POWs. There's that eruption of intolerance that sweeps over a nation at war. And many of us at home who can't or won't fight, look for easy targets here. Someone who has even the remotest relationship to the enemy becomes suspect. It's the war mentality, there are good guys and bad guys." Emotion now fills his voice. "I did that to my best friend. In World War II, when we were at war with Italy. I was about 8 years old, and a bunch of us in the neighborhood chased Sal Fertitta into his house. He was my best friend and I didn't have the guts to go against the rest of the crowd. I can remember Sal asking me if I would come in and play with him, because nobody else would."

On that Sunday morning Jack and I sat in our living room moved to tears, feeling a sense of helpless sadness for all the victims of all wars, those in combat and those sitting at home, wherever their homes might be.

When will we ever, ever learn. When will it ever end.

Flag Waving — Peace Weaving

No one wants another Vietnam, *ever*. No American wants to see the people of this country repeat the national disgrace of treating dedicated servicemen and women with the disrespect and contempt normally directed at traitors. And so, once the troops were committed to combat in the Persian Gulf, most people, those who believed in the war, and those who did not, tried to show their support for the warriors in whatever way they could. News of that support was ensured of reaching the military men and women in Saudi Arabia by way of newspapers, TV, as well as by snapshots and letters from home.

Morale on the home front was also important, displaying our colors helped to meet that need. During the winter of '91 yellow ribbons decorated trees, mailboxes, buildings, and car antennas. And all across the United States, American flags were displayed to bolster the spirits of those at home, as well as those on the desert battle-field.

It seemed to me that no flag pole went unused during the weeks of war, and many new ones were erected.

The ground swell of patriotism could also be heard during the winter of 1991. Our national anthem took on new meaning. From ice hockey games to the Super Bowl, to videos and CDs "The Star Spangled Banner" became the most popular song in the country.

As with most Americans I have my own very personal feelings about our flag, that involves experiences and teachings.

I am never unmoved by the flag, and the ceremony surrounding it. As a Girl Scout I was taught how to properly raise and lower the flag, without letting it touch the ground. As a reporter I watched as a human flag, with young people from all over the country, was constructed at Fort McHenry, the home of our national anthem. In Russia, I sat and listened as the Baltimore Symphony Orchestra played the Stars and Stripes Forever in a concert hall where the flag of the Soviet Union and the United States stood side by side.

I don't even try to fight back the emotion at times like these. As a very young woman I did try to cover up such patriotic displays of emotion. I don't anymore, because it's so much more than patriotism. It's pride and respect, joy and appreciation, and sadness, too, that the rest of the world can't experience what I do every day; to live and work, love and be loved in a country where one is not told that they *have* to respect the flag, and what it represents, and so, most of us do.

One of the things that the flag represents is our freedom to publicly disagree with our government. During the winter of '91 the flag also flew in the name of peace. War protestors carried it into the streets and waved it over anti-war rallies and demonstrations.

Two Baltimore women chose a quieter approach to display their disapproval of war. They designed and made "patches for peace."

Naomi Dagen Bloom, a 57-year-old social worker, got the idea for the patches when she saw a bed sheet being used as a sign hanging out of a window in the inner-city. Bold and black the letters simply spelled out . . . NO WAR.

Naomi's friend, graphic designer Sally Mericle, designed a 2½ inch rubber stamp which pictured the American flag, under it were the words "No War," then "S.O.S" (Save Our Soldiers).

Using bed sheets, the women personally stamped out thousand of the homespun patches, then handed them out for people to pin on their clothing. On January 19th, in Washington, D.C., they gave the pieces of "peace" cloth to 5,000 people, gaining national attention when they were featured on the MacNeil/Lehrer News Hour.

Naomi says, "The idea follows such traditional women's crafts as quilting," adding, "we see these patches as being as supportive as the yellow ribbons."

Naomi says she would never have been so public with her feelings and beliefs when she was a young woman, because then she felt the restrictions of living within the guidelines and views of her parents, and of conforming to what society expected women to be.

"Now," she says, "at 57 I don't give a damn what other people think of me and what I do. I only have to please myself, and of course my husband and children, and they support me and my causes."

At one time Naomi wouldn't have dared to even try and change the thinking of her family; now she is trying to change the thinking of the people of the world. To weave into war the idea that peace, understanding, negotiations might be a better way to deal with our differences than killing one another.

Thinking Brings Direction

I spent a lot of time during the winter of 1991 just thinking, about the war, my health, no work, not much money coming in, and what to do with the rest of my life.

Actually it was tempting *not* to think; to do anything but think. It was hard to keep myself from succumbing to the idleness syndrome; the debilitating disease of not having anything "important" to do, so you don't do anything. It was hard not to just stay in my bathrobe all day, lie on the couch in front of the TV, and let the broadcasters who *were* working tell me about the war.

When you don't have a specific job to do, it's hard not to just vegetate and wait for the phone to ring, especially when the doctors, and your husband, have told you to take it easy.

However, self-motivation, a personal trait that I was either born with or learned at an early age from my hard-working German father, overcame the idleness syndrome. Even under the influence of my medication, which left me lethargic, I felt that I needed to accomplish something everyday. I started writing again, even though it was difficult to concentrate.

Each day I'd set a goal for myself: to write a page or two, which usually lead to more. I'd straighten one room, sometimes just one table in one room. But I felt good about having achieved my goal for that day, no matter how small.

Then I began to think about finding some work that would pay me some money. I figured the phone would never ring if I didn't do something to stimulate calls. "I need to send out some letters," I told myself. "I need to make some calls of my own, set up some job interviews."

But I was getting ahead of my needs; first I needed to know, not only what I wanted to do, but where my abilities might be welcome.

TV is what I do best, but let's face it, with the emphasis on face, the chances of any television station in the country hiring a woman in her fifties are a lot slimmer than I am. Not that I would move to some other state, even if a job offer were made.

Actually there is a better chance of my being hired in the Baltimore/Washington area where I'm known, than anywhere else in the country, but the possibilities of even that happening get fewer as I get older.

No sense getting uptight and bitter about it, that's the nature of the business. When Jane Pauley starts to look old to TV executives what chance do *I* have?

Few women have been allowed to age in front of the TV camera, and usually the visible effects of aging have been camouflaged; by plastic surgery, hair coloring, and cosmetics.

No woman who looked like Charles Kuralt would be on the air. "Sorry Charlie" but you aren't on TV because of your beauty, you're there because, in my opinion, you're one of the best, if not the best, writer, reporter, and anchor the industry has ever produced. *But* if you were a woman, we'd never have seen how talented you are.

Don't misunderstand, age and appearance are also determining factors in the hiring, firing, and career advancement for men in television, but to a lesser degree.

Continuing to use Charles Kuralt as an example; I feel that if he were tall, thin, with a full head of hair, he certainly would have been chosen by CBS to replace Walter Cronkite, instead of Dan Rather. What the television executives ignored, with that decision, was that of all the people who filled in for Cronkite, before his retirement, Kuralt got the best ratings. In spite of that, the executives went with the person *they* felt would be more appealing to the viewers, primarily women viewers, between the ages of 18 and 45. I've always thought they were wrong in their thinking. I love to watch Kuralt, now and when I fit in that all important advertising age range. Obviously a lot of other women do too. He continues to be extremely popular whenever CBS allows him to broadcast. I'm personally grateful they have allowed him to continue with programs such as "Sunday Morning." My point is that if he were a woman I don't think he'd still be on the air.

At most local television stations the only older women you see on news shows are those hired to do "senior" reports, stories about much older people in nursing homes and senior centers. I find that as offensive as having women do only "women's" stories, or black reporters always doing the stories that involve black people.

Part of the shame of not allowing women to grow old and gray, while continuing to report the news on television, is the negative message it sends to young girls everywhere. The message being that this is a world that will love you only if you're young and beautiful, and will reject you when you aren't.

Television is a powerful force in affecting change. It should be setting responsible, if not popular, standards by the images it projects. And those images should be reflective of the society it serves.

If we were to judge our society by the people we see reporting the news, or hosting news and magazine shows, we would have to conclude that there are almost no women in America over fifty, and none with gray hair.

Okay — chances are that I won't be working in television on a regular basis, ever again. What else would I really like to do?

I get up and walk to the window to look outside. "If I never had to leave this farm it would be fine with me," I thought. "But unfortunately I'm not a farmer, I can't make any money here."

I put on my coat to go out and walk around the property. I always think better outside. I take a couple of apples to give to the horses. On the way to the barn, I take a bite or two from one of the apples, "That'll be my lunch," I think, trying to convince myself that I'm doing a good thing by going easy on the calories, and that I'm not really wasting the food budget by giving these apples to the horses, I'm just sharing my portion.

"Sassy," — short for "Sassafrass" — Emily's pony, has her head over the fence watching me as I approach. I give her the half-eaten apple, and pat her on the neck. "You're a smart pony. You know that? And so sweet." I wrap my arms around her neck and give her a hug.

"Sassy" is a large dark brown pony with a white blaze down her face, and markings like two white stockings on her hind legs. She has red highlights in her mane and tail that glisten in the sunlight, and she has the softest, most loving dark brown eyes that mirror her gentle and kind disposition.

I bought this pony for Emily at a horse auction during the summer of 1989. "Sassy" was in her late twenties, at the time, which is old for horses, so she went cheap. That's the only reason I was able to afford her. If she had been in her prime, a pony of her breeding and training would have cost anywhere from three thousand to five thousand dollars. I paid seven hundred. (It's not just people who are judged less valuable with age, is it?) But, it is precisely because of her age that this pony is priceless for a 7-year-old child. She is experienced, calm, quiet, and wise with an understanding about the ways of children.

All the grandchildren can climb on "Sassy" and she wouldn't think of doing anything that would hurt them. It is because of her age, and what that has done to form her character, that we love this pony so much.

I put my arms around Sassy and give her another hug. Seemingly jealous my horse, Jay Jay, nuzzles in, pushing Sassy out of the way. I reach in my pocket and pull out an apple for him. "You don't think I'd forget you, do you?" I say as he takes a bite of the apple cradled in the palm of my hand. "You're my boy, no one could take your place." I reassure, as if my horse can understand what I'm saying. Jay Jay is a big bay quarter horse, he's kind and brave, a companion and friend. We've spent many hours together, riding around the property, exploring the woods. We've come to trust one another completely. I think perhaps that's the most important aspect in any relationship.

I'm anxious to start riding again. The doctor said, "no riding," while I'm taking Prednisone, because that drug softens bones, and if I fell off I might suffer a severe break, or damage my back just in the course of riding.

I reach into my pocket to get an apple for "Lady," the little Shetland pony, and one for "Jenny," my daughter Marjorie's horse.

I think about spring with Marjorie, Emily, and me riding through the woods and perhaps Tommy bouncing along on "Lady." So far Emily and Tommy are the only two grandchildren who have shown an interest in horseback riding.

From the barn, I walk back toward the house, through the paddock gate, around to the south side of the yard, to check on the gold fish in the pond I dug last spring.

There are edges of ice around the pond. The bright green parrot feather plants, which were floating on top, are now frozen in place, locked in a state of stillness. The film of clear crinkly looking ice that has formed on the shallow end of the pond is about a half-inch thick. Under the ice, huddled among the roots of the plants, are the fish in an almost motionless state. At the deep end the fountain, which is a little boy on the back of a turtle with the water coming out of the turtle's mouth, keeps the pond from completely freezing over. It also circulates air through the water making it easier for the fish to breath.

This is the first winter for the pond, and I look everyday to make sure the fish are surviving the often freezing temperatures.

When the weather warms, as it occasionally does during Maryland winters, the fish become active, seduced by the warm sun and melting ice into thinking spring has arrived.

On this day I sit on the bench by the pond, watching the orange-gold of the fish waver, ever so slightly, under the frozen shield. It's like watching the fish through a frosted shower door. I hear the sound of a child running across the lawn behind me. It's Tommy coming from his house.

"Hi MeMe, are you home? Can I come to your house? Can I feed the fish?" Tommy doesn't wait for answers between questions.

"Yes, Yes, and Yes," I say quickly.

"What?" Tommy looks quizzical, staring directly into my face. "What did you say?"

"I said yes, I'm home; yes, you can come to my house; and, yes, you can feed the fish, if they'll come out from under the ice." I send Tommy into the house to get the fish food, and I resume thinking about what it is that I really want to do.

I want to stay home, I decide, work part-time; to go on working out of my house. I want to be able to take time out for the grandchildren, whenever they want to spend time with me. I want to hear what they did at school, as soon as they get off the bus, not an hour later, or a week later. I want to be there when they need someone to talk to.

We have this unique family compound, and I want to take advantage of it.

I want to be here when the children are little. I want to share a life with them.

I realize, somewhat sadly, that what I want to have with my grandchildren is all the things I missed with my own children, because I was too busy establishing a career, and making a name for myself. The most important name in my life now is MeMe.

The life I had six months ago is the life I want to continue. I don't want to go back to television; not full-time. I want to write, produce videos, and do more work on the radio. (Age doesn't matter on the radio.)

I'll be very happy if I can just make enough money to pay my bills and supply the grandchildren with such things as riding lessons, and an occasional ski trip. (I bet you never thought I'd want to do that again.) I don't need a lot of money, but I do need some. I promised myself a long time ago, when I was married to my first husband, that I would always find a way to generate my own income. I swore that I would never again be entirely dependent on a man, or anyone else, for my survival or personal pleasure. I must have my own money to meet my needs, or whims, without asking permission to spend it. (Of course anytime Jack wants to take me back to Bermuda I'll gladly be a kept woman for a week.)

"MeMe," Tommy calls, as he comes running out of our living room door, and across the screened porch. "The telephone is for you," he continues, as he runs toward me with the can of fish food in his hand.

"Did you answer it?" I ask, knowing that a three year old isn't the most reliable answering service available.

"Yes, I did," he bragged.

I go inside and pick up the phone. At least Tommy didn't hang up the receiver. "Hello," I say in a searching tone, wondering if the caller is still there.

"Hi, Susan, this is Bob Malzahn over at Baltimore Lutheran School. We've decided to go ahead with that recruitment video we talked about. We were hoping, if your company isn't in the middle of another project, that you could get started right away."

12 Spring 1991

You may see sunshine and
flowers, I see moonbeams.

Spring Preview

The first warm spring-like day of 1991, in Maryland, came during the first week in February. As a matter of fact there were several consecutive days above 60 degrees.

The grass started to turn green; crocuses pushed up through the softened earth. Farmers nearby began to plow their fields. The mud in the barnyard began to dry and pack under the horses hoofs. The goldfish darted around the pond with youthful energy. The birds began to sing, and the grandchildren hurried outside without thinking about coats or closing the door.

The bikes came out, the sand in the play-yard once again took on an irresistible quality for the busy little hands and creative minds of the children.

The sleds, snow saucers, and toboggans stood abandoned; lined neatly against the fence over by the hill.

Even without snow they would remain there until the middle of March. I learned many years ago that it was a waste of time, and perhaps asking for a blizzard, to put snow things away in February.

On that first warm day of 1991 Emily's thoughts were on her pony and going for a ride. Her mother, my daughter O'Donnell, had asked me to meet Emily's bus after school. O'Donnell had begun a part-time job at the hospital, and this was one of her days to work.

Emily leaped off the bus, her excited plea reached me before she did. "MeMe, will you bring "Sassy" in from the field so I can ride her? Please, MeMe, please?"

Of course I would. It was a pleasure to be outside for whatever reason. But to be helping my granddaughter enjoy her pony made it something I wanted to do as much as she did.

Tommy decided that he also wanted to ride, and his mother, my daughter Marjorie, was there to lead him around. In fact she led him out around the fields and through the woods, with Emily following along on "Sassy."

"When spring really gets here," I thought, "I can go with them, because I'll be off the medication, and back to normal." Instead, on that wonderful February day, I walked out to the ridge of the field, stood in the warm sunshine under clouds rimmed with pink, and watched the pony procession meander around the farm.

There are perfect moments in life that should be recognized as such, savored, and then stored away in our reservoir of remembrance.

This mental holding tank of good experiences and feelings can help refresh and nourish, and keep us going during those cold, dark, and often depressing times that are also part of life. By recalling those perfect moments, hope for similar times in the future seems reasonable.

That day was clearly one of those perfect moments; another came the following day at just about the same time.

It was late afternoon, all the children were playing out in the field that surrounds Marjorie's house. They were playing camp-out with a pretend campfire. I could see them from my screened porch on the south side of the house. A little later I noticed that Marjorie had joined them. The children were scurrying to gather large stones. Then O'Donnell came walking down the road which leads form her house, past mine, to her sister's. She was looking for her children, to see where they were, and what they were up to.

It was all too inviting; a beautiful day; my daughters and grandchildren all together in one spot, and it looked as if they were going to stay put for a while.

I walked out across the lawn into the field, around the embankment on which Marjorie's house sits. Marjorie and the children were building a real campfire. O'Donnell was sitting up on the bank watching. The children were excited and wanted me to know why.

"We're building a campfire, MeMe, a real one," Brian emphasized.

"Yeah," said Tommy, laughing and squealing as he jumped up and down.

"You want to come to our campfire?" Jay asked.

"Sure," I answered, pleased I was being invited, but knowing that I was welcome even without an invitation.

"I have two hot dogs," Marjorie said, "We're going to cut them into pieces so everyone can cook something over the fire. Do you have any?" she asked me, "or marshmallows?"

"No," I answered, "I don't have either, but how would you like a big pot of hot chocolate?"

"Yeah," the children screamed in unison.

I didn't have much milk so I made the hot chocolate with water. No one seemed to notice, or, if they did, they didn't seem to mind. The big pan of chocolate drink sat on one of the flat rocks that circled the fire. It bubbled and steamed, and the kids used a dipper to scoop it up and fill their cups. The children cooked their one bite of hot dog, savoring each blackened morsel.

"This is wonderful," I commented. "I haven't been this relaxed in weeks."

"I sure needed something like this," Marjorie said, "I'm glad the kids got the idea to do this."

The expression of contentment on O'Donnell's face conveyed her agreement that this was a perfect moment.

All three of us had been winter weary. All three of us were dealing with a medical problem, and stress of one kind or another. But on that afternoon none of us felt the effects of any problems.

The fire burned down to a warm glow, as the sun was setting behind us. To the east, out over the reservoir, up over the tree line, we watched as the moon began to rise into the winter sky.

Eleven days later the coldest weather of the winter clutched the northeast, and sent us back inside to build fires there. But the perfect moments from our few days of a February spring provided warm memories and hope for what lay ahead.

The Moonbeams of Spring

I have this serene feeling that it's going to be a good spring. I've been off the cortisone medication for a month now. There is every indication that the vasculitis of my brain has been successfully treated and eliminated. There has been no recurrence of the terrible headaches. In fact, I've had no headaches at all, which is most unusual for me. I think this must be the first month-long, un-medicated period I've lived through without a headache since I was a teenager.

Since the end of February the news has been all good. On February 28th, the same day that the end of the Persian Gulf war was being heralded on the front page of newspapers all over the world, in the TV column of "The Washington Post" it was reported that Jack Bowden had been signed to a three year contract by WJLA.

My husband was working full-time again. I could stop worrying about how much money I wasn't making. I could go on enjoying the lifestyle I had decided I wanted to live. The pressure to earn our living would now be shouldered primarily by Jack alone. I'd try to add to our income whenever I could, but it wouldn't be up to me to keep the bills paid.

My spring schedule is exactly what I wanted; a mix of profit and non-profit. I'm working on the video for the school, (whose principal had called). I have just finished writing several radio advertising campaigns with others pending. I have a heavy schedule of speaking engagements coming up, and several meetings that will conclude my work on the Governor's Task Force on Self-Esteem. And I'm writing.

With Jack working full-time, I'm free to do what I really want to do. I can re-discover the life I began to pursue 30 years ago, before I felt the need to be liberated. Don't misunderstand for a moment. I DID NEED TO BE LIBERATED. I wouldn't be the person I am today without all those years and experiences on the job, away from the home. I wouldn't even have met Jack.

But now I've been liberated again, this time from a misconception which was created by many of us women in the 1960s and '70s. Women who led the way into the work force with diaper pins holding up our sagging hemlines, (we didn't have time to mend them).

We were determined to do it all, with the emphasis on career. The message we mistakenly sent by our example was that the only really interesting, productive, women are the ones who have jobs *outside* the home.

We have now learned that women have many choices, all contributing to the many dimensions of the middle-aged woman of this decade. I know some women in their fifties who are just now beginning to pursue careers. These are women who *did* stay home with their children, and now want to experience life "on the job." Some are just now entering college, to prepare for those jobs. I think that's wonderful. I know one couple where, previously, the man never lifted a finger around the house. The woman in this marriage waited on her husband for 30 years, as if he were King Tut. The "King" is now retired and she has gone to work. He does all the housework and cooking. She comes home each evening to dinner on the table, prepared by her husband.

Jack and I used to share the dinner duties, but with him driving back and forth to Washington every day, getting home so late, I've been fixing dinner every night. And I'm now finding that I'm enjoying taking over the responsibility for this meal; shopping, trying out new recipes; arranging the centerpiece for the table.

There is one exception to this picture of domestic bliss. I still dislike housecleaning and find it to be of very little reward. If you keep the house clean and neat all the time no one notices; they take it for granted. But if you let the house get dusty, and disorderly *everyone* notices. There is no praise when you need it, but lots of criticism when you don't.

No matter how much someone loves life on the home front, getting out occasionally is a must. Several nights after Jack had signed his contract, we decided to go out to dinner, at our favorite restaurant, to celebrate. In an effort to conserve and cut back our spending, we hadn't dined out for months. The budget was forgotten that night, as the celebration ensued. I was celebrating his new job, he was celebrating my reprieve from ill health.

Over champagne cocktails, Jack took my hand in his and said, "I'm so happy to have you well again. I don't know what my life would be without you. Look, I won't be able to take a vacation until next fall, but in September how would you like to go back to Bermuda?"

He knew what my reaction would be, my eyes filled with tears as did his.

"You won't mind being a kept woman?" he joked.

"I think I'm starting to really like it," I kidded back.

We drove home in a torrential downpour. The wipers, even on high, couldn't keep up with the volume of water pelting the windshield. It didn't change my exuberance or appreciation of life as it was now unfolding. Jack and I went to bed very happy and very much in love.

In the middle of the night our dog "Blaze" began whimpering to go out. She does this at least once a night. Those of us with a little age on us can appreciate her need. Jack and I share the nightly chore of letting Blaze out: whichever one hears her is the one who gets up. On this night I was the light sleeper. As is the routine, I opened the sliding glass door, that leads from the bedroom to the screened-in porch, shuffled across the porch to open the screen door to let Blaze go outside. Normally, I barely open my eyes, as I plod though this nightly ritual. This night was different.

The rain had stopped. The three-quarter moon shone almost as brightly as the full moon several nights earlier, when the Gulf War was declared over.

On that night, as I watched the news on television, while cooking dinner, I could see the full moon outside my kitchen window.

Then, in reports from liberated Kuwait City, that same moon was behind the reporters and the celebrating people of Kuwait. In other pictures it created an orange glow behind the city of Baghdad and provided a strong light for shots of Washington, D.C. That one hugh circle of light making the world seem so small, and so much brighter.

On this night a mist was rising up out of the valley. It hung just below the tree line. The branches of the trees, seemingly growing out of the fog, silhouetted against the moonlight sky, appeared to be a forest of fantasy.

I followed Blaze down the porch steps, deciding to wait for her to return from her walk. Usually I go back to bed, and try to sleep while half-listening for her whining and pawing at the screen door to be let in again.

I stepped onto the soggy ground and felt the grass and mud compress under my feet. I love to feel with my feet. It's a childish delight that I've never outgrown. There is something wonderful about walking barefoot on a hot dusty road; the sand at the shore; the mud and slippery rocks in an icy cold stream bed, or across a freshly cut lawn. Jack's never been fond of the grass clippings, sand, and God knows what else I drag into our bed. But, you know something? I think he's even getting used to that. This man who grew up in the city and lived there until his mid-forties, when he married me, has become a real lover of country living.

I leaned back against the porch railing to savor the night and to think about all the good things that were happening in my life. Jack's new job; my being able to do what I want, to stay home, work out of my house, to see the grandchildren almost every day. My daughters seem happy. Their husbands are doing well. *AND*, Jack and I are going back to Bermuda. I shook my head, not in disbelief, but to make sure it wasn't hurting. I've started doing that since being off the medication. No, not even the slightest hint of a headache, even after drinking champagne.

I'm one of those people who believes I can talk to the good Lord, anytime, any place, and be heard. I think perhaps I truly believe, as my father did, that I'm closer to God with my hands in the soil, planting a tree, than in the most ornate cathedral.

But I think I want to go to church this Easter Sunday to give some official prayers of thanks. I hope our good friend, Father Fred, doesn't suffer a heart attack from the shock of seeing me there.

I looked up at the moon, and in a kind of lopsided, one-eyed way, it seemed to be looking back at me, or was that a wink I saw?

13 Making Every Day Count

During the summer of 1991 J was
determined to make every day count.
J might have fifty more summers, but
J lived that one as if it would be my last.

Reunion

In June we held a reunion that brought together some of my son's former friends. They came from as far away as Colorado; some of them hadn't been here since Jody's funeral in 1977. The mother of my son's best friend, Eddie, organized the reunion and did most of the work, but it was held here on the farm where we have lots of space for that type of event. Besides, I really wanted to see Jody's motorcycle buddies in this setting again, after all those years.

These were kids who had raced "moto-cross" with Jody. They were all teenagers then and most had also ridden in the memorial race we held after my son's suicide. "The Jody White Memorial Moto-cross" was held for a specific reason and offered a special trophy. The prize was given not necessarily for the winner but for the rider who displayed the most perseverance during the race; the rider refusing to give up, in spite of difficulties or mishaps out on the track.

As I told the young riders before that race, "Jody would never have given up in a motorcycle race. It was when things were the toughest, out on the track, that he raced his hardest. And if he didn't win that race, he realized there would always be another race when he might win. If Jody had understood that life must be faced the same way, and offers the same continued opportunity for success and happiness, he never would have killed himself."

Those boys and girls of the '70s came back as men and women of the '90s. All are now thirty or thirty-something. They are taller, filled out, and mature. Some are married with children; some not. The males who wore shoulder length hair during the hippie era, now have very short haircuts; several guys are even balding. But I had no trouble identifying any of them, however, they had trouble recognizing each other. They'd look and question, say a name, and embrace. The only tears I experienced that day were tears of joy as I watched them recapture the closeness they had felt as kids.

My friend Marge, Eddie's Mom, had worried the reunion might be hard on me; make me sad, wondering what Jody would have been like at this age and wishing he could be there. Although I don't go through a day without wishing that Jody was still alive, I did not feel sadness or resentment on that occasion. I was just happy to see Jody's friends who had meant so much to him, and to me, when he was alive.

None of us at that reunion were locked in the pain of the past, or the agony of what might have been. We were remembering the good times we once had, and enjoying the happiness of our present lives.

The irony for Marge was that Eddie wasn't at the reunion either. He now lives in Florida and had been planning to drive straight through to Maryland the day before the reunion. But as he started out his truck broke down. He couldn't get it fixed and it was too late to make flight arrangements. Marge and her husband, Dick, Eddie's stepfather and the only Dad Eddie ever knew, were extremely disappointed that their son hadn't been a part of this rare and special occasion. Though missing Eddie, they too were deeply touched at seeing "the kids" all grown up.

Dick had served as a surrogate father for many of these kids, including my son. He took them to motorcycle races, and water-skiing on his boat. Dick was their mechanic, mentor, and father confessor. He was there for the boys when no one else was.

At the end of September Eddie did come back to Maryland — for the funeral of his beloved stepfather. Dick died of a stroke, complicated by the cancer he had been battling for a year. He was 58 years old. As Marge and I hugged at the funeral home, with tears streaming down our cheeks, we spoke as one: "I'm so glad we had the reunion *this* year."

At the reunion, three and a half months earlier, I had talked to Dick about making the most of every day; not putting things off. We were standing by the outdoor grill. Dick had a can of beer in one hand, and using a long handled spatula, he was turning hamburgers with the other. His youngest grandchild, age 5, was playing nearby. He was watching her with much more interest than he was the food on the grill. "These grandchildren are the greatest, aren't they?" I said. He looked over at me, raised an eyebrow, and smiled as if there were no words to express how much he agreed. "The greatest," he finally muttered, as if saying a prayer of thanks.

Dick had been operated on for throat cancer, part of his tongue had been removed. Even though the prognosis following the surgery had been good, you could see he didn't have the strength and stamina he once had. He was thin, and his speech was thick. However, his good natured, strong-willed passion for life had not abated. He didn't talk about dying, he only talked about living.

I began to share some thoughts that I sensed he'd understand. "You know, after what I went through last winter with the vasculitis, I've really started trying to make every day count. None of us knows how much time we have left. And not only do I want to enjoy whatever time that is, I want to give my grandchildren something to remember that will help shape their lives in a positive way. I hope they'll not only remember me, but carry on where I leave off. I want to set an example that I'd like to see them follow. I like to think that when I'm gone they'll recreate what I did for them with their children and grandchildren. I figure the most valuable thing I can leave behind is a legacy of love."

Dick looked at me as if I'd been reading his mind. His eyes filled with tears. I felt as if I were staring into his soul, and at that moment, I knew that he knew he didn't have much time. Dick handed me the spatula, put down the beer, and walked over to pick up his granddaughter.

Summer Camp

In July I held a camp for my grandchildren. I looked at my calendar, blocked off every Wednesday and Friday, and organized "MeMe's Camp" for all six kids.

I explained to my daughters, and grandchildren, that this was not a baby-sitting service. I didn't want the kids to feel that they had to come to camp, but if they did come I wanted them to know that they would have to participate, cooperate, and obey the rules.

They all came; 8-year-old Emily, the twins, Brian and David aged 6; their cousin Jay, also 6; Jay's brother Tommy, who would turn 4 during camp on July 23rd; and the littlest camper, Alexander, just 3.

Camp began at 9 o'clock with a campfire breakfast, and concluded at 3 o'clock, after swimming. I told each child to bring a backpack containing a change of clothes, long pants, a bathing suit and towel.

On the first day of camp I was ready by 8:45, and eagerly awaiting the arrival of my campers. Smoke from the campfire circled up through the branches of the maple tree. Bubbling hot chocolate in a big white enamel pot sat on one of the rocks surrounding the fire. I had carefully placed seven cinder blocks, evenly spaced, around the campfire. On one I had written "MeMe." I would let each of the children use the black marker to write his or her own name on their cinder-block seat. I sat on my cinder block staring into the fire, enjoying the morning quiet, and a hot cup of coffee, listening for the voices that would tell me the children were headed my way. Finally they came, and they seemed just as excited as I was.

"I want to sit on that seat." "I want to write my name first." "Where should I put my stuff?" "Can I have a cup of hot chocolate?" "What's for breakfast?" "Can we go swimming first?" They all spoke at once, their questions overlapping.

"Hold on for a minute," I interrupted, "First you'll each write your name on your seat; then we'll sit down, have a cup of hot chocolate and talk about what we're going to do at camp, and when. Whatever we do we'll do as a group. When it's time for riding lessons, or swimming, or anything else, we'll do it together. You can't go off by yourself and play in the sandbox. Camp is organized; we have a schedule, and we're *all* going to stick to that schedule. Do you understand?"

Six little heads bobbed rapidly, and in unison, with a certainty of commitment I felt sure couldn't last. (Remember those old plastic figurine dolls with loose heads? They were popular during the '60s and '70s. Most of them depicted football players of varying teams. It was as if someone, with six of those dolls in the back window of their car, had suddenly hit the brakes.) Whether the children really understood what they were agreeing to or not wasn't important. Truth be known, I wasn't real sure what I was getting into either. I figured things would develop as we went along. It was enough that they shared my enthusiasm. I began by explaining the plans I had made.

"The first thing we're going to do each morning, before we eat our breakfast, is go to the barn and feed the horses. The reason we do that first," I explained, "is because horses and other pets like dogs and cats, can't take care of themselves, and we must think of them first and feed them before we feed ourselves."

My camp was not just going to be for fun and recreation there were many lessons I hoped to pass on; lessons I'd learned from fifty years of life, and as a child from my mother and father, such as feeding pets first. To this day the first thing I do in the morning is feed the horses, and make sure they have water, and in the evening I again take care of the horses and feed the dog before I start fixing our dinner. And I told the children that this way of thinking should also be applied to *people* who need our help and care; friends or relatives who are sick, elderly, or in the hospital. And then there are the less fortunate, the poor and disabled in the community who should have our concern, care, and support. I hope to reinforce that point someday by taking them along when I take clothes or food to a shelter or crisis center, but that wasn't part of camp.

Camp consisted of all the things my grandchildren are lucky enough to have available all the time, like horseback riding, swimming, and hiking, but in a structured form. When we began, some of the children were comfortable on horseback, others were timid. The same with swimming. No matter what their ability in the various areas, I asked that each of the children try what I was asking them to do, at least once. To my surprise they did, because it was part of camp. Before they would have said, "I don't want to do that," and just sat still staring at me, or run off to do something else. I was delighted, but astounded, that my plan was working. For example, I was teaching them to swim under water; to dive down on one side of the shallow end and swim across the bottom to the opposite wall of the pool. I demonstrated what I wanted them to do, and then asked them, one by one, to do it, beginning with the children I knew would be most comfortable doing it. Emily, the oldest and a good swimmer, was first. When I got to Brian I wasn't sure what would happen. Brian is one of those children who hates to get his face wet. When water is accidentally splashed in his face he always rushes out of the pool, grabs a towel to dry his eyes, while complaining about the person who splashed him.

"Brian, you're next," I called. Brian jumped into the pool, dove down to the bottom, and swam to the other side. When he came up there was a smile on his face, and mine. He forgot all about the need to get a towel to dry his eyes. Instead he dove down again and swam back.

The riding worked the same way. Jay and David, who had decided at age six that they weren't interested in horseback riding, and never would be, were riding with confidence and enjoyment by the end of camp. It remained me of my stepson, Christopher, and tennis.

Christopher went to a summer day camp one year when he was about seven or eight. The first day he came home complaining that he didn't want to play tennis. He said it was hot, tiring, and dumb. His father and I said, "Try it. It's part of camp, so you have to do it." He's now one of the best tennis players I know, and he loves the game.

The other part of "MeMe's Camp" that pleased me was "the daily word." Each day I chose one word that we'd talk about. We did this after lunch, and before swimming. I had the children write the word on paper, with a definition, after I had looked up the word in a dictionary and read the definition there. I then had them write the opposite word and it's definition. Words like, polite and impolite, friendly and unfriendly.

A couple of times we even did some improvisation; acting out the meanings of the words. The children loved doing that, especially the negative words such as impolite. If you think your child isn't controlling his or her behavior, just as we adults do, give them permission to be impolite, and you'll see how rude they really can be.

I wasn't sure the children would retain, or put into practice, the information discussed at these daily word sessions, but I thought it was worth the effort. I was particularly doubtful about the two youngest children understanding what was going on. Then, one morning, Tommy pushed Alex out of the way so he could get his hot chocolate first. Three-year-old Alex got up off the ground, walked straight over to me and said, "MeMe, Tommy was very impolite." We all agreed, and Tommy was asked to apologize to Alex.

The close of camp was a triumphant occasion for us all. We planned an evening campfire, inviting the children's parents and their other grandparents to come for dinner, and the closing ceremonies. It took us most of the last day of camp to get ready. On large pieces of brown paper, grocery bags opened up, the children wrote the words they had learned. We strung bailing twine from the pine tree to the lilac bush. Using clothes pins we hung up the sheets of paper containing the words, and also the pictures of camp activities that the kids had drawn. Using cinder blocks and long boards, we made a bench for our guests. The children wrote the names of their parents and grandparents on the board so that everyone had a special place to sit, just as they did. The bench read: Marjorie — Jody — Jackie — Ne Ma — O'Donnell — Steve — Mom Mom — Pop Pop. An extra cinder block was put next to mine for Jack.

For dinner we had hot dogs, cooked over the fire, sweet corn from nearby Farmer Sill's, and tomatoes from O'Donnell's garden. Ne Ma brought a big pot of baked beans, which she calls Indian beans, and Mom Mom brought coffee cake. I made each child responsible for an adult, explaining that they, the children, were the hosts of this party, and they had to make sure that their adult was served dinner and something to drink. They would also have to check on them from time to time to see if they'd like something more.

The kids were superb. They were polite, responsible, considerate, friendly, thoughtful, sensitive, and patient; putting into practice all the positive words we had discussed during camp, and impressing the somewhat shocked parents and grandparents who were not used to these, or any other children this age, acting in such a cordial manner.

With dinner concluded, it was time for the closing ceremony. The sun had set and darkness was rapidly closing in around us. Several more logs on the fire built the flames and provided the only source of light.

In the glow of the firelight the children locked arms and sang our camp song. The song, which I had chosen, is from the movie "Puss'n Boots." The children's voices were clear and strong as they sang, "Everybody needs somebody, that is clear to see. Aren't you glad we've got each other, that's how it should be. I got you and you got me, and just between the two of us. I'm for you and you're for me, and that's between the two of us." If it hadn't been dark the children would have seen that the adults were watching, as they listened, through very misty eyes.

Next came the awards presentation, a surprise for the children. They had not been told that there would be awards at the end of camp. I didn't want them doing things, or competing against each other just to get awards. However, I did want them to know how proud I was of their participation and accomplishments.

I bought six tiny pewter cups, and on each I had engraved, "MeMe's Camp 1991," under which was engraved the reason for the award. As I gave out the cups I explained why each camper was getting that award, praised their performance, and called them up to get their trophy.

Emily: *Most Helpful*. Alexander: *Best Sport*. Brian: *Most Advancement*. David: *Most Cooperative*. Tommy: *Most Willing*. Jay: *Best All Around Camper*.

Camp was a success. It proved to me the importance of structure and organization in a child's life. It proved to me that lessons don't have to come from someone outside the family, like a school teacher, for the children to take it seriously.

I'm as pleased and proud of the way "MeMe's Camp" turned out as anything I've ever done. I don't say that without taking into consideration the award winning television reports and documentaries I've done, the books I've written, the speeches I've made, or the panels I've chaired.

Upstairs in my office, on the walls, are awards and citations from The Associated Press, United Press International, civic organizations, charities, the Governor and the Mayor. Downstairs, on my kitchen wall, next to the big white enamel pot I used for hot chocolate at the campfire, is the most meaningful certificate of accomplishment I've ever received. It's parchment paper glued in scroll-like form to two sticks. It hangs from bailing twine. The hand written words read: "I'll never forget camp." It's signed Jay, and dated 1991. It was a present for my birthday on August 4th, four days after the close of camp.

If I had been working for the television station during the summer of '91, and making a good salary, I probably would have *sent* my grandchildren to camp. I would have said to my daughters, "I think the kids could use a camping experience, let me pay for it." The children might have gotten the same kind of experience, but I would have missed out. By having more time than money I gained some wonderful memories, while, according to Jay, my grandchildren experienced something they'll never forget.

Giving Thanks

On the Sunday before Thanksgiving my friend Marge asked me to go to church with her. It had been just two months since her husband's death. She was arranging the cornucopia on the alter. Dick had done it in past years. Marge was carrying on, not just with that tradition, but with life. I wanted to be there for her.

The morning began unseasonably warm, but by eleven o'clock, a strong, cold wind out of the west, bringing dark, winter-like clouds, moved across the area, dropping the temperature rapidly. Leaves swirled at my feet as I started up the steps of the Deer Park United Methodist Church. Even though I had driven past this church hundreds of times I had never been inside. It is a tiny country church, originally built as a log cabin in 1877. It was rebuilt in it's present form in 1923. The form-stone exterior and plain concrete steps reveal the era of it's renovation, and the fact that the congregation had no extra money to spend on show.

Inside, two modest stained glass windows frame the plain wooden altar and altar rail. One window pictures the Holy Bible; the other the dove of peace. Folding chairs are set up to the left for the choir; a small organ is on the right. The upper walls and ceiling are of ornately molded metal, painted the color of butter cream and white. They resemble the sides of an elaborately decorated wedding cake. The lower third of the walls are encased in walnut paneling, warm and dark with age. A total of sixteen wooden pews, eight on each side of the center aisle, hold the church family. The numbers are few, about fifty in all. There is one infant, a dozen older children, and then there are parents, grandparents and great-grandparents.

Before the service a little girl with long curly hair, no front teeth, and wearing a brightly flowered dress, runs excitedly up and down the aisle. She stares at me from every angle, giggles, and runs back to her friends. Marge gives me a questioning look. "She's too young to remember me from television," I whisper. Finally, the little girl runs back, and comes into the pew where Marge and I are sitting. "Are you Emily's grandmother?" she asks. "Yeah," I say, too loudly, as I recognize her as one of Emily's school friends, whom I'd driven home from Brownies. "That's nice," I thought, "to get the same reaction for being someone's grandmother as I used to get for being on television."

I liked that. I really liked that.

I feel a sense of peace and contentment envelope me as quiet settles over the congregation. Even the children become silent.

The organ begins, the voices join in the singing of the first hymn, "We gather together to ask the Lord's blessings."

At the conclusion of the hymn the pastor asks the parishioners to share with the rest of the congregation some of the blessings they've recently received; to praise the Lord's works; to give thanks out loud.

Some speak, but most sit in silence, as I do, reflecting on personal blessings. There are so many things for which I have to be thankful this year. I hear myself whisper, "Thank you, dear God."

The pastor adds his thanks for that particular Sunday morning. "I'm thankful," he says, "for that strong wind out there. It's blowing all the leaves off my lawn and down into the woods."

We all laugh. I think about last year, being sick and not being able to rake my leaves. With the help of my stepson, who's back home from California, we've almost finished the job this year. And I could have done it alone, because I'm well. I did make it to see another fall. "Thank you, dear God."

The call to worship is the first Psalm. It concludes, "For the Lord knoweth the way of the righteous: but the way of the ungodly shall perish.

I think, "If ever there were good people, righteous people, it is the people in this church. Perhaps that is why their church has not perished." I think, "God may be helping them, but they've done a lot to help themselves."

It is only through dedication and sacrifice that this small congregation has kept this sanctuary alive. Because of their work and commitment, because of the struggle, they're here most Sundays to enjoy the fruits of their labor. Would they be here; would they care, if they hadn't made a personal commitment that involved time as well as money?

The words of the pastor came back to me from Dick's funeral service, which wasn't held in the church because of it's small size. It was held, instead, at the funeral home. The pastor spoke of Dick's commitment to this church.

"Dick gave so much of his time to our church. He helped with the electrical wiring; he helped with repairs. I'll always remember, and hold dear, the mental picture of Dick up on the roof putting on new shingles."

My eyes move slowly from one parishioner to another. Would this church matter to them if they hadn't done without in other areas of their lives so that they could support the church?

When things are easy we do tend to take them for granted. When we think we might loose something precious, or when we do loose something precious, we start to think about what really matters in our lives.

As I look around it seems to me that my life now is very much like this little church; simple, honest, unpretentious; without wealth, but with deep meaning and a great deal of hope.

Heading into the second century of my life, I realize, with all my heart, that time is the greatest gift of all. The greatest gift we can give, or get. No matter how much money we have it can't be used to enrich our lives if we don't have time.

Each day does count, and is filled with precious gifts, often unexpected. It is those daily gifts that make up the treasure chest of years we call our life.

Conclusion

It was warm for December 7th. The sun shone brightly on the nearly empty beach. Sea gulls were bathing in a gently rippling tidal pool; fluffing their feathers, and dunking their heads, undisturbed by the two humans invading their privacy. A little farther down the beach, at the edge of the ocean, a sea gull stood on one leg, pecking at the other. As we got closer I stopped and noticed that the other leg was broken. I dropped to one knee to look more carefully. A sympathetic moan slipped out of my mouth. Knowing I couldn't help, I rose to walk away. Looking back I felt guilty that I couldn't impose my domestic powers on this wild bird.

"How do you think a sea gull would break a leg?" I asked Jack with concern.

"Waterskiing?" he answered irreverently. I laughed out loud, as I always do at his silly jokes, then pushed him away as a reprimand.

Jack, on vacation from the television station, had suggested that we spend a couple of days in Ocean City, Maryland. He didn't need to do any arm twisting to get me to go along. We don't get much time together now. What time we have is precious.

Jack's work days are long, and tiring. Just the commute to Washington, D.C. is an hour and a half, each way. During the week he's rarely home before eight, eighty-thirty; often later, and he has to work many weekends. That's not a complaint, he loves reporting and anchoring the news, and he does have a job. So many other people don't, in this year of the deepening recession. The television industry has not been excluded from budget cuts and layoffs. High salaries have been cut; secure jobs have been lost. Being employed in 1991 is a blessing, no matter what one's job or profession.

I feel as if I should be doing more to share our expenses, but free-lance jobs and video production work are way down. I keep thinking I should try and find a full-time job, any full-time job. Recession aside, after more than twenty years of working outside the home, having a career, the guilt of having "dropped out" is hard to fight. The mind set that taking care of the house, farm, and family is not *really* working keeps invading the comfort of my choice to stay home.

We women have been well conditioned, over the generations, to view our roles of wife, mother, grandmother, and housekeeper as insignificant; not very important in the big picture of society's progress and productivity. For years, it was mostly men who fueled that falsehood, keeping us humble, and grateful for the financial support we though we could never achieve on our own.

When my mother died the man who had written the obituaries at "The Baltimore Sun" for decades headlined her obit as follows: "Former Teacher, Dental Assistant Dies." My mother taught school for only a few years before quitting to get married and have a family. She never returned to the teaching profession. She became my father's dental *receptionist*, not assistant, because he insisted that she do so. It helped him, and saved money. She was never paid a salary in the more than thirty years she did it. She was a loyal, devoted, loving wife and helpmate, but she was not a trained dental assistant.

A loyal, devoted, loving wife does not make headlines, even in obits. By most male standards, there must be a more widely accepted accomplishment than that, in a woman's life, to justify a write-up when she dies.

And, now, we women are making the same kind of judgements about our own successes, and those of other women. Even women, such as I, who have achieved career success, good incomes, and positions of power; who have proven to ourselves, our mates and all others that we can succeed outside the home, have this feeling that we must justify ourselves when and if we go back to being *just* a homemaker.

"I know," a friend said to me, "that you're taking care of the house and the farm, and helping out with the grandchildren. But what kind of *work* are you now doing?"

Jack fully appreciates my role at home, understands the work involved, and does not resent being the primary source of income. I'm the one who is bothered by it.

Even though I'm the one shopping for, preparing, and serving the food, I find it difficult to ask for *his* money to buy it. I work on feeling less guilty, while looking for ways to bring in a little more money on my own.

However, I do think we're all going to be doing with less money in the years ahead. I believe that the effects of the recession of '90-'91-'92 will continue well into the 21st century. I think that most of us will be very reluctant to return to the irresponsible spending of the '80s, even if we have the money to do so. And I don't think many of us will. I think most of our children will be the first generation in a long while who don't achieve a more affluent lifestyle than their parents.

More grandparents are going to have to help care for their grandchildren, as *their* children struggle just to make ends come close to meeting. It's a valuable and worthwhile service that we do, helping to shape the next generation. Like all other volunteer jobs it's one that cannot be measured in a monetary way.

I realize there are many women, now in their fifties, who feel very differently about this. These are women who are just beginning to experience their independence. They just got out of the house and you couldn't get them back in there with a team of recruits that included Erma Bombeck, Martha Stewart and Barbara Bush.

Two women I know, who feel this way, have just decided they want a divorce after 30-some-years of marriage. There aren't other men in their lives. They just don't want to be married any more. They don't want to be obligated to a man any more, for any reason. They will do with less money, and fewer luxuries, for more freedom.

I'm glad I had my career when I did. I'm glad Jack and I fell in love when we did, otherwise we probably wouldn't have appreciated what each of us brought to the marriage, and to each other. If we had married in our twenties rather than our forties, I might now be struggling for the same kind of independence, identity, and individual recognition that could cause me to push him away.

I'm also glad that, as a 50-year-old grandmother, I feel the same kind of support and admiration from my husband, that I felt when I was forty and we shared an anchor desk at the television station.

I'm glad that I've been able to achieve the self-confidence and self-esteem, in my fifty years, that will allow me to grow old without torment.

Our arms locking us together, Jack and I walked down the beach as one. We are so lucky, so lucky indeed.

I'd like to be able to end this book by saying that I'm sure I'll live happily ever after, from this moment on. But if there is one thing I've learned in 50 years it is that "happily ever after" does not happen in real life.

And so I'll tell you that I'm going to live happily until the next crisis occurs, and that once again I'll do everything I can to get through it, because I have also learned that my granddaughter is right, moonbeams *do* come at dark times.

There are two white chairs,
down by the sea,
one for him,
and one for me.

We sit in silence,
my love and I,
our heads tilted back,
as we look at the sky.

"Do you think about dying?"
he asks without pain.
"Not much," I answer,
"it seems so in vain."

"We've had a good life,"
he says with some thought,
"but I'd like to have more
of this joy that you've brought."

"I know," said I,
with reflection of time,
"and I worry about
leaving the kids behind."

There's not much we can do
but enjoy every day.
"I love you," he said,
"come what may."

September 1990
Somerset, Bermuda

About the Author

SUSAN WHITE-BOWDEN is a prize winning journalist, receiving awards for her work in television, radio and newspapers. For 22 years she was a reporter — anchor for WMAR-TV in Baltimore, where she established a popular feature called "Susan's People."

Susan now produces videos for WHITE-BOWDEN ASSOCIATES, a company she co-founded with her husband, Jack Bowden.

A long time volunteer, Susan is the former chairman of The Maryland Governor's Task Force On Self-Esteem.

Susan has achieved national recognition as a lecturer on youth suicide prevention and surviving loss. In recent years the subjects of her lectures have been expanded to also include: Women in the Media — Balancing Home and Career — Volunteerism — Self-Esteem and the Important Role of the Grandparent.

When listing her priorities Susan puts her family first and as she reveals in MOONBEAMS COME AT DARK TIMES her grandchildren now receive much of her time and attention, as well as her love.

The farm where Susan lives, works, and writes is located in Finksburg, Maryland.